Miles and Miles

Miles and Miles

by

MILES KINGTON

HAMISH HAMILTON
LONDON

First published in Great Britain 1982
by Hamish Hamilton Ltd
Garden House 57-59 Long Acre London WC2E 9JZ

Copyright © 1982 by Miles Kington

British Library Cataloguing in Publication Data

Kington, Miles
  Miles and miles.
  I. Title
  828'.91407 PR6061.I/
  ISBN 0-241-10901-9

Typeset by Saildean Ltd
Printed and bound in Great Britain by
Richard Clay (The Chaucer Press) Ltd, Bungay, Suffolk

For Alison Rice
who bullied me into writing
most of these pieces, and is thus
the best kind of editor

The Perils of Roller-Skating

I have recently taken up two new sports, roller-skating and ankle-spraining, in that order. I am getting quite good at both.

The easiest way of taking up roller-skating is to have children who want to roller-skate and to feel that you'll be damned if you'll be outdone by them. The easiest way of taking up ankle-spraining is to be challenged by your son to a race round the rink. You end in a dead heat and fall over in a heap together. He gets up and rolls away. You get up and fall over. You have sprained your ankle.

Both sports are quite cheap, as far as equipment goes. For the first you simply need a pair of skates, though it's also advisable to have gloves, elbow pads, knee pads, bottom pads, skiing cap, the T-shirt of any American university, traffic indicators, a loud horn and a sleeping bag into which you can crawl if you fall over. The second is even cheaper; a bandage and a walking stick will get you through, unless you start with master classes in which case you will need a pair of crutches.

Don't forget, by the way, that all sports are divided into two categories. There are the sports which intoxicate by the sheer speed with which you glide over a hostile element (roller-skating, windsurfing, sailing, skateboarding, hand-gliding, surfing and skiing). And there are sports which involve a great deal of effort and no gliding (jogging, bicycling, boxing and ballet).

The trouble with the first category is that by the time you have started to get any good at it, it's desperately out of fashion. I have known people who woke up one day with an urge to windsurf, bought a windsurfer at midday and read a piece in their evening paper called 'Whatever Happened to Windsufing?'. It wasn't actually a windsurfer; it was a frisbee; but the message is the same.

Ankle-spraining never goes out of fashion.

The technique of roller-skating is very easy, and can be summed up in one sentence. Whatever you do, make it look on purpose. For instance, it's all very well when people tell you that you just push with the outside of your skate and glide along. *You* know that. Your mind knows that. *Everyone* knows that. But your feet don't know that. Your feet think that the idea of roller-skating is to go in a different direction from your body. So you fall over. *Make it look as if you're practising falling over.* Are you tottering and shooting your feet out in all directions? No – you're practising disco dancing.

Also remember that roller-skating is dependent on centrifugal force. This is a scientific principle which states that the worst roller-skaters go to the outside and the best to the inside. Well, it's more common sense really. The worst will hang on to the wall, the next-worst want to be within reach of the wall or at least able to hang on to those hanging on to the wall, and so on, till you reach the middle. That's where the best skaters are. Unfortunately, there is no room for the best skaters to skate in the middle so they roller-disco-dance instead, and good luck to them.

By some curious law of science which no one has ever explained, the best roller-skaters are all black. Don't get me wrong. I'm not a racialist. There are also some very good white roller-skaters. I have nothing against white people. Gosh, I'm white myself. But I can't help noticing that the best are all black and the worst are all white. I think skating rinks ought to hire at least one very bad black skater just to encourage the others but this may be perfectionism. All I can say is that if you want to roller-skate, and haven't yet made up your mind whether you want to be black or white, I think you ought to think seriously about being black.

The sheer exhilaration of gliding along on skates can hardly be described, and the same goes for the wonderful feeling when you're ankle-spraining – that sort of breathless feeling of not being able to move at all and suddenly noticing all the little things you take for granted, the blueness of the sky, the singing of the birds, the vast distance from your bedroom to the lavatory and the little details you'd never noticed before in the carpet, probably because you'd never lain full length on your carpet before.

If you are going to buy a pair of skates, remember that there are two different kinds. There's the kind which looks as if it was made out of Meccano and can fit any kind of shoe by a sliding contraption in the middle. And there's the kind which is made by the skateboard industry since the bottom fell out of skateboarding, and features wheels of four different colours, a brake block in front, a truck devised by the American aerospace industry, and boots left behind by the ice-skating boom of 1973. Next year they are going to produce a model which dispenses ice cream and receives Capital Radio.

When I started writing this piece, skating was still in fashion. I cannot accept responsibility if it has gone out of fashion by the time you read it, but remember: anything that goes out of fashion will always come back. The last time roller-skating was in fashion was in the 1950s, and if there is anyone in your office who looks forty-two and a half, always stands in the corner at office parties and blushes if someone stares at his tie, you can bet your bottom dollar that he is an

3

expert skater. I predict that roller-skating will be back heavily in 1998.

And this year? Well, it's difficult to say. But I think ankle-spraining might catch on in a big way. If, this time next winter, you see people with crutches equipped with coloured skate-wheels whizzing down your local pavement, don't forget I told you so first. I shall be ready. I have been practising dancing on crutches for two weeks already.

Rock of Ages

You may remember my admitting once that I could jive after a fashion. And by gosh, it's come in useful. I was one of the lucky horde who got tickets for the *Record Mirror's* 25th Birthday Party in Covent Garden. A quick sum will tell you that *Record Mirror* was born in 1955 (wrong actually; it was 1954 but the party got sort of postponed from last year) and the evening was devoted to 1950s culture. Fifties music, Fifties food, Fifties drink, Fifties dancing. Super.

Unfortunately it also involved Fifties costume. 'Come dressed in 1950s style', the invitation said sternly, rather like a sergeant-major telling you you're in the army now, so stop slouching around, lad! Only it was the other way round and we had to start slouching around, 'cos you're in the 1950s now. Well, it was all right for some lucky folk who haven't changed their style of dress since 1959 – motor-bikers, ageing rockers, merchant bankers, etc – but I'm sort of stuck in the mid-Sixties and don't look right for either 1980 or 1954. But I rooted around in the wardrobe and found an old duffle coat, a raggedy scarf and a pair of shoes with 1950s dust on.

'Just right,' I told the wife. 'I'll find a CND badge from an antique shop and I can go as an Aldermaston marcher. I know I didn't march in the 1950s, but it's never too late to make a protest. We have still got a bomb, haven't we?'

'If you think I'm going to dance with an Aldermaston marcher,' my wife said, 'you've got another think coming.'

I had another think, and ended up wearing jeans, lumberjack's tartan shirt, white T-shirt underneath, tough boots, and a chunky metal bracelet that looked as if it had dropped off the underneath of a British Leyland truck. I also forced grease into my hair, swept it back with a heavy duty horse comb and found the start of a small bald patch I had hardly suspected. I looked either like someone who had failed the auditions for *Seven Brides for Seven Brothers*, or a Canadian lorry driver. But after half an hour of striding round elbowing people out of the way (this is my family I'm talking about – we hadn't left for the party yet), I began to feel my way into the character. Real tough. Narrowed eyes. Widened shoulders. Swaggering like a grown-up John Travolta. Certainly a fitting escort for my dear wife, who had reappeared in sandals, dayglo-green ankle socks, sweet flared frock and the clean, healthy look of Debbie Reynolds.

The crunch came when we got out of our taxi in Covent Garden. I was wrestling in my pockets for some money (how on earth do Canadian lorry drivers ever get anything out of their pockets?) when my wife whispered in my ear: 'You've just dropped a pound note and one of those men picked it up and kept it.' I looked round. There, just walking off, were two rockers, looking meanish. They were both smaller than me, admittedly, but they were over five foot taller than me when you added them together. Normally I'd have calculated quickly that it wasn't worth getting into a fight for a rotten old pound note, but this wasn't normally and I wasn't normal; I was a real tough number with a real bit of diesel pipe hanging round my wrist. So, much to my own surprise, I heard myself saying, 'Hey! I'd like that pound note back, please.'

They turned and looked at me. They looked at each other. One of them said, 'You what?'

At this point I should have said, 'It's all right, fellows, I'm just a free-lance journalist dressed up as a receding Canadian lorry driver, ha ha, keep the money, would you like another pound note?'

But instead I snapped my fingers imperiously, did one of those little beckoning motions with the hand that always look so good when other people do them and said, 'Come on! Which one of you has got that pound?'

And after a moment's hesitation one of them dipped into his pocket and silently handed the note back to me.

The party, though good, was a bit of an anti-climax after that. I was totally surrounded by other lorry drivers and Debbie Reynoldses, and it's hard to stand out from the crowd if you're dressed as an extra. But the brush with the two rockers had taught me a valuable lesson; if you dress up as something, you *become* that something. It's not just that other people are fooled by the costume – you yourself are fooled as well.

There's a character in an Aldous Huxley novel who does the same thing. Until halfway through the novel he has been a mild, unassuming, withdrawn chap, the kind who holds doors open for other people at department store entrances and never even gets a thank you. Then he buys a large false beard and immediately becomes a commanding, impressive bloke – the kind that other people listen to, other women fall for, other men hold doors open for. His voice even becomes deeper and grander. Ridiculous, I thought, when I first read it. Now I can see that Huxley knew what he was talking about.

The same thing is true of judges, policemen, soldiers, ticket inspectors, or indeed anyone in a position of authority. They are all engaged in a perpetual fancy dress party, in which we pay respect, not to the man inside the clothes, but to the clothes themselves. It is reported that when they were shooting *Oh What a Lovely War!*, they had to dress hundreds of extras in privates' uniforms, and hundreds of others in officers' clothes, and that when they took breaks for meals or rest periods, the men dressed as officers all stuck together, the men dressed as privates drifted into another group *and there was no mixing between the two at all*.

Scary, when you think about it. In California, they even tried an experiment with student volunteers acting out a prison scenario. Some were put in prisoners' clothes, some dressed as warders. They called off the experiment hastily after several days when the warders started acting with real brutality towards the prisoners, even though they were all friends in everyday life.

Yes, on the whole it was nice to get out of my disguise and back to real life. Took me six days to get the grease out of my hair, though.

My Brothers, Roddy and Dai
J. P. R. Llewellyn's own story

Not many people know there are three of us Llewellyn brothers. That's because only two of us do the kind of thing that gets people famous. I just play rugby. I'll probably never be famous. So I'm grateful for the chance to tell my exclusive story, and I quite understand that I probably won't get paid much, if anything. Because I'm not famous. Pardon? That's quite enough about me? It's Roddy and Dai they want to know about? OK.

As a boy, Roddy liked playing with dolls best. Dai liked playing with girls best, and their fathers often came round to complain. I just liked going out in the mud and getting cold, dirty and wet; even then I must have known I was going to be a rubgy player.

The three of us had an ideal childhood – we hardly saw each other at all. For another thing, Father was always away in Helsinki with Foxhunter and the horses, or so he told Mother. 'A likely story!' she would snort, but then she never read the sports pages.

One day when there were all six of us at the dinner table – Father, Mother, Roddy, Dai, me and Foxhunter – I remember Father asking us what we were going to do if we ever grew up.

'I'm going to fall in love with a beautiful Princess and live happily ever after,' said Roddy, always the romantic. 'Don't be stupid,' said Father. 'Dai?'

'I'm going to wait till Roddy finds his Princess and then sell his story to a Sunday paper and live richly ever after.'

'Clever. J.P.R.?'

'I want to be picked for Wales,' I said.

'I didn't know Wales had a show-jumping team,' said my father.

'No, Father – *rugby*,' I explained. 'It's a game where you have to carry a ball and grab chaps round the knees and cripple them if the ref isn't looking.'

'Sounds bloody tricky on horseback,' said my father.

I realised my father would never understand. My brothers weren't interested in rugby either. Roddy spent most of his youth blushing, singing and gardening. Dai couldn't get interested in anything that didn't involve girls or champagne. 'Silly sort of a game,' he said to me one day after I'd been practising tackling Foxhunter for two hours. 'Why not get the servants to do it for you?'

Dai was engaged to three different heiresses at the time. He had just turned thirteen. He used to tell me that sex was great fun, but from his description it sounded just like scrummaging and twice the work.

Roddy was getting more and more romantic. He came to me one day and told me he was in love. I asked him with whom. 'Oh,' he said. 'Do you have to be in love *with* someone?' Even I

8

knew that. I was in love with the Welsh XV at the time.

At fifteen I had a trial for Llanelli. My rucking, passing and running were fine, but I failed the drinking and unarmed combat tests and the Welsh accent interview. My father said it was about time I went out into the big world and became unemployable like my brothers, but I begged to be sent down the mines so I could get picked for Wales.

'No need for that, boy,' he said. 'Plenty of coal out in the stables. You can have some for your birthday.'

Roddy was still very shy as a young man and became engaged to himself several times, though he often broke it off as he found himself difficult company; he told me he sometimes sat by himself and wondered what he was really thinking.

Dai was getting engaged all the time, but one day he 'phoned up in excitement and said: 'I'm *really* getting engaged this time, J.P.R.!

'You mean, you're going to settle down as a married man?'

'No, no – I'm going to settle down as an engaged man. That way you can have all the joys of married life and all the freedom of bachelorhood. Don't forget that some classes of society remain engaged for years.'

'That's because they don't have enough money to get married.'

'Precisely. Can you lend me £5?'

Still keen to play for Wales, I learnt a Welsh accent, see, didn't I, well then boyo, but the funny thing is that both my brothers have achieved their ambition and I still haven't played for Wales. I've only played for Aberpool 3rd XV, actually. But I'll say this; I've always played rugby like a gentleman. Till last Saturday, that is, when I finally went berserk at putting up with so much rough play. Before I was sent off, I'd maimed three people, half-killed the ref and attacked my own captain. I've just had a letter from the authorities saying I shall have to be banned for the rest of the season, but I'm almost certain to be picked for Wales next year.

Growing Pains

The care, maintenance and decent burial of house and office plants is made far too complicated by the amount of books about them. Especially as all the books list about 200 of them, none of which looks like the one you've been given. So, to help you, I have devised an entirely new classification of indoor plants which reduces their number to ten and enables you to identify any one at a glance.

1.   The Last Minute Birthday Present, or African Violet
This is instantly recognisable for its masses of green leaves and small coloured bloom. The bloom dies the next day but the leaves go on for ever.

2.   The Architect's Drawing Plant, or Pseudoplasticus
You know those tall, lifeless green monsters that architects stick in their ideal drawings to make a place look lived in? They have now managed to breed them in real life. You can spot them at once; they look as if they are made from green plastic. They should be polished once a day, and sandpapered once a month. (Experiments are also under way to breed the *people* seen in architects' drawings, who never drop litter and have no faces.)

3.   The Shrinking Violet, or Anorexia Nervosa
This spindly, sad, skeletal plant starts out quite tall and gradually gets smaller and smaller, by dropping leaves and branches, until it vanishes completely. It doesn't much like heat, cold, dark, light, food or water.

4.   The Nut Tree, or Palmus Miniaturus
These are generally grown from pips or seeds left over from fruit salads or steak and avocado lunches, and can be spotted instantly through their complete inability to produce nuts, fruits, or indeed flowers. If ignored for several years, they may grow into Architect's Drawing Plants.

5.   Last Year's Bulb
This non-flowering plant is the only one in nature which grows

bent over with a rubber band round it. The leaves eventually
turn a beautiful yellow, which is a sign that it is asking to be
thrown away.

6. *The Incredible Creeping Ivy*
Any plant which grows down rather than up can be classed as
an ivy. It grows out as well, spreading fast when you're not
looking but staying absolutely still when you've got your eye
on it. It likes to spread over unanswered letters, vital missing
files and out-of-date cheques. Its leaves are highly poisonous,
though nobody knows how this was discovered.

7. *The Travelling Flower Arrangement*
A colourful, attractive, mixed growth which appears myster-
iously in many offices on Monday morning and vanishes again
the next weekend, if it's still alive by then.

8. *The Climbing Office Plant*
Anything which climbs up a stick in a pot is one of these.
Many of them seem to suffer from vertigo or oxygen starvation
or something and peg out at about two feet above sea level,
which is why you see so many pots in offices with just a stick in
them. Unless, of course, people are taking the easy way out and
just planting sticks.

9. *The Yoghurt Pot Plant*
A pleasant, light green growth exactly the same size as a
yoghurt pot, though there is a larger version called The Double
Cream Pint Pot Plant, which is much rarer owing to the price
of double cream. They both thrive on crumbs, biscuits and
elevenses.

10. *The Temp Secretary Bloom*
Any plant which does not come into the first nine categories
can safely be classed as one of these, no matter what shape, size
or colour they are. They are always left behind by that girl who
came in for three weeks, remember, and then vanished to Spain
and we found she hadn't been doing any of her letters, just
hiding them in her desk, goodness, Mr Whitgift was angry, but
we hadn't the heart to throw the plant away.

Why Your Plant Isn't Looking Well
It was thought until recently that plants were damaged by
either over-watering or under-watering. It is now known that
plants can be simultaneously over-watered *and* under-watered.
Most pots are boggy and swampy for the first two inches down,
then bone-dry underneath. The plants are suffering because

11

they are puzzled and do not know what is expected of them.

If you are giving your plants plant food, stop. If you are not feeding them, start immediately. This is based on the theory that whatever you are going, it is bound to be the wrong treatment. Basically, what house plants like is *neglect*; this may kill a few weaker growths, but many house plants will emerge from a bout of forgetfulness and starvation even tougher and more determined to outlive you.

How To Write A Bestseller

More and more books are being published these days, but fewer and fewer are being written. Not by the author, anyway. Most books these days are too full of photos to allow any words (glossy books) or too full of drawings (children's books). The rest are all written by anonymous teams of researchers, sub-editors, assistants and other badly paid contributors. Except of course those that are written by dead people. The ace example is the *Country Diary of an Edwardian Lady*, half of which was someone's (let's face it) not very interesting diary and the other half of which was (be honest) rotten poetry copied out from other dead people.

So if you decide to get involved in books, don't muck around at the bottom level, where all the work is done; get straight in at the authorship level, where it will all be done for you. The only thing you will have to do yourself is the introduction, if you can't get a member of the Royal Family to do it for you, and this can be dashed off in a week or two.

Remember that by law certain things must always go into an introduction, rather like details on a French wine label.

1) You must mention your long-suffering wife or husband. If you haven't got one, someone else's will do. If you don't know any wives or husbands that you like, make one up.

2) You must say that nobody in the book is based on real

people. As all people in books are based on real people, this may seem odd, but it's just a protection against libel.

3) You should always end by saying, if possible, 'I am very grateful to all those who have helped me; all mistakes, of course, are mine.'

4) If you mention people, be grateful to them. Try not to say: 'I would also like to mention Professor Dundas of the Economic Centre, who was unfailingly bad-tempered and usually absent; the few facts he gave me all turned out to be wrong.' This creates a bad impression and a libel suit.

The introduction to your book will vary somewhat according to what it's about, so here is a collection of samples, one of which is bound to be near your kind of book.

For cookery books
'I am extremely grateful to all those famous chefs and hoteliers who know so much more than me and unstintingly gave of their time and recipes. I am more than grateful to all those cookery writers whose books are now out of print and copyright, and from which I have unstintingly stolen. I am eternally grateful to my family, who unhesitatingly offered themselves as guinea pigs for all my experiments, and especially to my husband, who has done all the real cooking in the house for three years.'

For practical books
'Although this book is aimed at the layman and written in easily understood prose, it should also appeal to the expert, the student, and d-i-y man, the practitioner, the professional and the housewife. It aims to be, not just a small basic manual, but also the most comprehensive work ever written on the subject. There is no reason or excuse why every single inhabitant of the British Isles should not buy a copy.'

For wine and spirit books
'This book could not have been written without the willing co-operation of certain large international drink combines, who gave me lots of money and whose products I have warmly recommended.'

For scholarly works
'Those who helped me are far too numerous to mention, but I

13

should just like to single out (here insert about a hundred names which should include not just people who helped you, but the people who wrote the book, people you want to buy the book, people who might help you with your next book and just people you owe dinner to).'

For travel books
'Manganesia is still a remote country. It is inaccessible, dangerous and inhospitable. The people, though friendly and warm, are very suspicious of strangers and liable to have them for dinner. I am accordingly very grateful to those experts who have made a special study of this country and gave me unstintingly of their time to fill me in on this wonderful land, which I would have visited personally if the weather had not turned a bit dodgy and if I had not been so busy selecting photos for the book.'

For biographies
'I could not have written this book without the unstinting help of the University of Nebraska, who own many letters written by this wonderful man of letters, or indeed without the assistance of his widow, who burnt far more.'

For a bestseller
'My thanks are also due to the *Sunday Times, Observer, Telegraph, Express* and other papers too numerous to mention, who have agreed to feature extracts from this book in the fortnight before publication instead of finding stuff of their own, and to pay me for the privilege! Some people will never learn.'

Laying Down The Law

In these drifting days of gloom and disillusionment, we need rules and principles to cling to. Wouldn't it be nice, I sometimes think, if a modern Moses came down from a modern Mount Sinai holding some new commandments for our times – at least, until the lawyers got hold of them and turned them into legal language so that only they could understand them. Well, I'm glad to be able to tell you that a modern Moses has appeared. His name is Paul Dickson, he is an American and he has just published over here a book called *The Official Rules*. There are about 2,000 rules in the book and I can understand every one of them.

You'd probably recognise some of them. There is Sod's Law, which says that buttered bread always lands butter side down. There's Parkinson's Law, which says that work expands to fill the time available. There is the Peter Principle, which says that people are promoted to the level of their true incompetence, and so on.

They are in fact the laws which govern real life, as opposed to science. Science will tell you what happens in thermodynamics, but it takes Meditz's law to tell you that, no matter which tube train you are waiting for, the wrong one always comes first. Go to Newton for the facts on gravity, but go to McGovern for the truth about jobs: the longer the title the less important the job.

Another law seems to be that if a man thinks of a law, he will write a whole book to explain it. Parkinson did; Peter did; so we should all be eternally grateful to Paul Dickson for having resisted the temptation to do anything but just list these laws. Dickson himself has supplied a good law of his own; that the size of the shaving cut you inflict upon yourself is directly proportional to the importance of the event you are shaving for.

But the more I think about these laws, which sound so thoroughly modern, the more I realise that they are not unprecedented. They have been around for a long time. Until now, however, they have been known as proverbs. Murphy's First Law, for instance, says that if anything can go wrong, it will go wrong. Which isn't so very different from saying that you shouldn't count your chickens before they are hatched. And proverbs, like these laws, are very gloomy. Don't put your eggs in one basket. An order that can be misunderstood will be misunderstood. A newspaper article about errors will contain errors. You can take a horse to water, and so on.

The basic difference between proverbs and these laws, is that

15

proverbs are gloomy in advance. Look before you leap, is a gloomy foreboding. But the laws are gloomy in hindsight. They assume that the worst has already happened, and they are trying to explain it, which may say something about our modern state of mind, especially when we are so gloomy at the moment that you get the impression people actually want World War III to happen so they can get it over with.

Perhaps the trouble is that a great deal of these laws are just different versions of Murphy's Law: if a thing can go wrong, it will go wrong, and the trouble with that is that it doesn't help you. What we really need are laws that work, and which you can use in everyday life. There is a well-known law, for instance, which I didn't find in this book, to the effect that the amount of time spent in committee on a problem is in inverse relation to its importance. Put another way; a committee will vote through a bill for £1,000 in one minute; it will take an hour to argue over a bill for £1. Again, the more willing people there are on a committee, the less will get done.

Nor do I find Kington's Law in this book, which deals with the phenomenon known as perforation. The law states: If a line of holes is punched in a piece of paper, that line of holes becomes the strongest part of the paper. If you just tear idly at a sheet of stamps, it tears across the Queen's head, not down

16

the perforation. If you pull at a cheque, half of it comes out of the cheque book. As for lavatory paper ...

The one thing I have found is that you can make these laws work for you. I have found, as a bicyclist, though I am sure motorists will agree, that when you approach green traffic lights they turn red just before you get there. If on the other hand you want them to turn red so that you can change radio station or, as I haven't got a radio on my bike, put on your gloves or bicycle clips, then they stay green. This happens too often for it to be a coincidence. So what you do is this; if you desperately want the lights to be green, you say to yourself: 'I hope they turn red so that I can blow my nose or get out and put the aerial up.' To spite you they stay green, which is what you wanted in the first place. Believe me, it works. I just can't get it short enough to turn into a proper law.

There are various other laws which I have formulated in life. One is that when you move house everyone sends your cheques to the old address and your bills to the new address. Another is that if you are travelling in a car and wish to point out something of sensational interest to your fellow passengers, it will have completely vanished by the time the first passenger has turned in the right direction.

But then I am sure that everyone has a good law waiting to get out. If you have a good law which you want everyone to know about, send it to me and I'll let people know about it, if it's good enough. Just put it in an envelope and send it to this address. Soon it will be returned to you marked 'Not known at this address'. That's one of the rules of life, I'm afraid.

Travelling Very Slowly Through Peru

I was probably better prepared for the Day of Action than any man in Britain. I had just returned from South America, where every day is a Day of Action, or in Spanish, 'mañana'. I knew before I went, of course, that it was the Spanish style to put off to mañana anything that could be done today, knowing all along that tomorrow is the real deadline. You make an appointment to meet someone at 10.30am. You turn up at 10.30am. They do not turn up. You ring them to find out what happened. The answer is that they forgot it was 10.30am and would six o'clock this evening be all right? Of course it would, So you turn up at 6.00pm. They do not …

The more honest kind of Peruvian, or at least the one who knows a bit more about European habits, will make allowances for your quaint Western customs. He will say: 'Shall we meet at Peruvian time or English time?' By which he means, shall I turn up when I can make it or on time? And if you want him to be on time, he will make a special effort and hardly be late at all. And yet none of this is really because he is inefficient or lazy – it genuinely is because the rhythms of Latin American life are as different from ours as are the rhythms of their music. The essence of life there, or at least in Peru, is improvisation; you make the rules and then you bend them to fit.

You notice it first in the way they drive. I don't mean in their speed and aggression, though there are obviously a great many amateur Grand Prix drivers around, but in their unspoken Highway Code. One rule of the unofficial Highway Code is that if more cars are going one way than the other, then the majority is obviously entitled to the other side of the road and the minority will find itself being pushed on to the pavement by oncoming traffic. It works, too; rush hour in Lima is crowded but it never comes to a standstill as in London. Again, if the lights are against you but there is clearly nothing coming the other way, you go straight through the red lights – even when I was being driven somewhere in Lima by a British Embassy official, I found that he had adopted local rules, and we sailed blithely through ten crossroads in a row with the lights at red, though being British he did slow down first to have a look.

In Britain, again, a car horn hooted is a car horn hooted in anger. It's reserved for a necessary occasion. In Peru they hoot the whole time but never crossly – it's merely a signal that you are coming, a kind of automatic piece of machismo. It could mean almost anything specific – that you are about to crash a red light, that if you don't get off that zebra crossing you will die, that you are going to overtake, that you have just seen a friend on the pavement, or that you haven't hooted for about five minutes and you just want to see if the horn still works.

The trains in Peru hoot most of the time too, but here for a different reason. The railway lines are built mostly through high, mountainous areas with few roads, so naturally the Indians use them as places to walk along. Every time a train hoots it's because the driver has just seen some Indians on the line ahead, often driving llamas or sheep along. They have plenty of time to get off, because trains don't go much faster than twenty mph, but nobody wants to run a llama over as they suddenly become very costly when compensation is being sought. The only problematic spot on Peruvian railways is a tunnel; there just isn't room in a tunnel for a train *and* a herd of llamas, which is why all tunnels bear a skull and crossbones notice; a kind of government health warning for people who can't read. Not that there is really much risk; there's only one passenger train a day on most of the lines in Peru, and if you make sure you know when it going to pass, you're safe. Unless it plays a dirty trick by coming at English time instead of Peruvian time.

The first train I took in Peru ended up by doing neither. It left punctually enough (a hangover from the days when the British ran it, less than ten years ago) but was behind schedule ever after. It crept up through the Andes, going higher and higher towards the top spot on any standard rail system in the world – 16,000 feet, higher than Mont Blanc. At every station we stopped at, all the passengers got out, and all the Indian vendors on the platform got in, selling the local speciality – ponchos, maybe, or fruit, or fresh fried pork, or sweet potatoes, or chewing gum. The horn hooted, and panic ensued as everyone resumed their original position.

But there came a time in the late afternoon, when we were twenty miles short of our destination of Huancayo, drifting gently through a valley full of maize and potatoes and eucalyptus trees, with snow-capped Andes in the distance, when the train stopped on a bridge. Peruvian stations are often pretty small, but never small enough to fit on a bridge, and the passengers soon sensed that something was wrong. I had been sitting in the open air, on the steps (something you can't do on Inter City), idly watching an Indian woman in the fields with her baby strapped to her back and reflecting how far she was from our mechanised life. Together with the other passengers I wandered up to the front to try to find out what was happening. What was happening was that the driver was fiddling with every moving part on his engine and not telling anyone what was wrong.

A farmer came past, driving a bull. It wouldn't go under the bridge. Sweating and cursing, he started chasing it. Some of the passengers went to help him. The Indian woman from the field came up to have a look, suddenly seeming not at all far from our broken-down way of life. A few passengers gathered their luggage and departed for a main road visible in the trees. The sun got lower. The driver reappeared and asked if anyone in the crowd had a knife he could borrow. I threw him up my penknife and he vanished back inside the engine. More passengers left the train. A Peruvian came back from talking to the fireman. 'He say, driver very stubborn man. He say he can fix train. But he can't. He say, it best you walk.' 'But he's got my penknife.' Shrug. 'You get it back, you walk.'

So I did, feeling very far from mechanised life and down among the Indians now. I wonder how they feel about the blessings of European civilisation? The Incas had a perfect civilisation in which everything and everyone worked. Along came the Europeans, bringing trains that broke down, red

20

lights that were ignored and appointments that weren't kept. I'd sue, if I were an Inca. But being sensible people the modern Indians try and keep outside the Peruvian economy as much as possible. They build their own houses out of sun-baked mudbricks; they make their own clothes out of their own llama and alpaca wool; they grow their own food; and if they want to move something, they carry it on their backs. For a while I believed that Indian women had actually developed broad, sticking-out bottoms on which to rest their loads till I realised that they have actually improved on nature by wearing very bulky quilted petticoats.

I got to Huancayo eventually. The brother of the man who ran the local garage had a car which in return for a few elderly Peruvian bank notes he was willing to turn into a taxi. Later in the evening I found most of the passengers from the train in the one decent restaurant in Huancayo, and we compared notes on how we had all got there. It was a very Latin American occasion; the normal had failed to happen, which was the usual state of affairs. As I said, every day's a day of action there. And I suddenly found myself liking it a lot.

Skate Debate

Will Britain's roller-skaters be going to Moscow or not? That was the decision facing the British Roller Olympic Commmittee last night when they met in the bar of Streatham's Hot Wheels roller palace. And they voted overwhelmingly in favour of the motion 'That in no way do we not want to be involved'. Nobody seems to know this morning, though, if that means they're going or not. A transcript of the meeting doesn't seem to help much, either ...

Chairman: Well, I think everyone knows everyone here. Kev, Percy, Winston, Mo and Battersea Betty. So let's get down to the nitty gritty. Do we go to Moscow or not?

Kevin: I thought we were going to Hammersmith.

Chairman: Yeah, *tonight* we're going to Hammersmith. I'm talking about this *summer*. Do we go to Moscow this summer?

Kevin: What's wrong with Majorca?

Chairman: Look. It's the Olympics I'm talking about. Do we want to make a protest or don't we?

Percy: That's not the point, really, is it? I mean, the point really is do we even want to go to Moscow? I mean, it's hard enough getting to Hammersmith, what with the traffic. And from what I hear Moscow's pretty dead in the evenings.

Betty: Yeah, but look at it this way. I've been practising six hours a day for Moscow. Know what I mean?

Percy: Yes. You'll be too tired to go when the times comes.

Betty: No, I mean, this is my big chance. By the time the next Olympics come round I'll be a granny with a mortgage and everything.

Winston: By the time the Olympics come round again they probably won't even have roller skating. It'll be wind-surfing or frisbees or something.

22

Mo: A lot of us have made a lot of sacrifices to get this far, you know. Like giving up jobs and things.

Kev: A lot of us didn't have jobs anyway.

Chairman: And to be fair, we didn't even know till yesterday that there was skating in the Olympics.

Percy: And the dates of the Olympics clash with the big outing to Aylesbury.

Betty: We could get the date changed.

Chairman: Well, let's vote on that, then.

Mo: Oh, that's going to look pretty good in the papers, isn't it? 'The British Roller Committee voted last night to go to Moscow if the date of the Aylesbury outing could be changed.' We'd be a laughing-stock.

Chairman: OK, I vote we don't vote on that then.

Betty: How do we get to Moscow, anyway?

Winston: It's sort of down the M2 and ask again at Dover.

Percy: *Dover*? That's miles. It'll cost a packet to get there.

Betty: Then why don't we skate all the way to Moscow? You know, Britain's plucky team dances its way to Moscow and all that. Cheaper, anyway.

Chairman: We haven't even decided if we're going yet.

Winston: I once went to Dover on a school outing. It was incredibly boring.

Percy: Let's be honest, Aylesbury isn't much shakes either.

Kevin: Who goes skating for the scenery? I mean, if we did, we'd all be going to Woburn Abbey, wouldn't we?

Mo: My friend Sharon went to Woburn once. She said it was really nice and lots of space to skate where they had all these old stones.

Chairman: Well, we could all go to Woburn instead of Moscow.

Kevin: *Look*! The British public is waiting for us to give them a lead, and all we do is natter about going to Woburn. As I see it, it's very simple: do we refuse to go as a protest against Afghanistan or don't we?

Betty: I've got nothing against Afghanistan.

Kevin: Against the Russians being there, twit-face.

Betty: I thought the Russians were in Moscow.

Kevin: They're in Moscow *and* in Afghanistan. They invaded the place. Don't you ever read the papers?

Betty: It wasn't in *Roller News*.

Kevin: God give us strength.

Betty: So if we refuse to go the Russians will be so upset they'll leave Afghanistan, right?

Kevin: Something like that.

Percy: I think if we are going to make a protest, we ought to protest against something we really feel deeply about. Like the price of new wheels.

Mo: Or the traffic getting to Hammersmith.

Chairman: Right, then. We have a new motion. That we refuse to go to Moscow as a protest against the price of wheels and the problems of getting to Hammersmith.

Winston: It doesn't sound right to me yet.

Chairman: Then flaming well think of something better.

Winston: All right, I will. How about we ask the Russians to change the date of the Olympics to avoid clashing with the Aylesbury outing?

Mo: Has anyone got the Russians' address?

Barman: Telegram for you.

Chairman: Telegram? Wow. I never got a telegram before. How much do I owe you?

Barman: It's free.

Chairman: No kidding? Hey, I must send some myself.

Percy: Open it for heaven's sake.

Chairman: Right, hold on, I am. It says, it says ... TO BRITISH ROLLER OLYMPIC COMMITTEE WE URGE YOU TO APPEAR AT GAMES STOP KILLANIN.

Mo: Killanin? Where's Killanin?

Keven: Not where – *who*. He's a bloke. Lord Killanin. He's an Irish peer.

Chairman: I didn't know they had peers in Ireland. I mean, it's a republic and everything. How do they have lords?

Kevin: Well, I don't know. Maybe they were left over from the Norman Conquest.

Percy: Maybe they made people Irish lords if they wanted to get rid of them. Like sending them into exile.

Chairman: Well, I still think it's a liberty having lords in a democracy.

Kevin: OK, then, if you feel so strongly about it, we could refuse to go to Moscow in protest against Irish lords.

Mo: I don't want to hassle anybody, but if we don't go soon, Hammersmith will be closed.

Betty: I don't want to depress anybody, but my feeling is that this committee is incapable of actually getting to Moscow.
Chairman: Well, sod it, let's not go then.
Percy: Right. We have a motion now. This Committee says Sod it, Let's Not Go Then.
Kevin: We've got to make a decision that *means* something. In no way do we not want to get involved.
Chairman: Seconded.
Everyone: That's cool.
Kevin: OK. Anyone for Hammersmith?
(*The debate continues*)

Peddling Wheels

The gangs of bicycle thieves at present infesting London have become even more daring. Until recently they had contented themselves with stealing bikes left behind by their owners, but now bikes are not even safe when the owner is sitting on them. In Oxford Street, for example, pick-pockets are now operating on bicycles. They come up behind bicyclists at traffic lights and before they turn green, neatly take away all the contents of their back pockets, shopping baskets and side panniers. If they don't have time to take everything, they simply follow their victim to the next red lights.

Mr Peter Archangel of Croydon fared even worse.

'I was out on a tandem with my fiancée Irene,' he reports, 'and we had drawn up at the crossing of Tottenham Court Road and Charing Cross Road. After we started again the pedalling seemed much harder, so I turned round to remonstrate cheerfully with Irene, but she was gone, nowhere to be seen. She'd been stolen in broad daylight. If the thief should read this. I'd like to urge him to return her. She was not of great financial worth, but she had great sentimental value for me.'

Some gangs have become even more daring, and more

skilled. Mr Reg Roberts of Esher had his bicycle stolen from him when he was on it. During the fifteen seconds he waited at Oxford Circus, he felt himself being very lightly lifted in the air and lowered again – so softly that he fancied it was the air shifting in his tyre, or the saddle springs easing. But when he came to start again, he found he was standing in the road with no bike. When he tried to pedal off, he fell nastily.

'This is an exceptionally skilful gang', says Inspector Derailleur of the Bike Squad. 'Most bike thieves are happy just to take the back half of the bike at lights. Over 1,000 back wheels and saddles have disappeared this year alone. May I urge all cyclists who stop at red lights to chain their bike securely to a post or railing till they go green? Better still, go by Tube or bus.'

But what happens to all those stolen half-bicycles? Latest theory is that they are being shipped to Holland to be repainted and turned into unicycles. But who is buying the unicycles?

'Everyone is buying unicycles!', claims Adrian Wardour-Street, head PR man of Friends of the Wheel. 'Roller-skating is old hat now; unicycling is where it's at. All the top people and trend-setters are one-wheeling their way to work!'

It must be a very exclusive trend, as no one has yet been spotted unicycling.

'Put it another way,' says Adrian. 'Although no one as yet is unicycling, if we say that they are loudly and often enough, they'll start, mark my words. This is how trends are born. And my goodness, this *is* a trend. One-wheeling is the safest, funnest, quickest way to travel. I'd do it myself except that I can't get hold of one. But as soon as the country is flooded with cheap unicycles from Holland, nothing will be able to stop the one-wheelers. It's going to be a monster trend, believe me. Probably by this afternoon, I'd say.'

What to wear while unicycling? That's the problem which Suzi Frisbee has been tackling for her women's wear page in *Natty Trends*. And the surprising answer is – almost anything.

'Cycling has always been a fashion hassle for the ladies,' says Suzi, in real life the living-in companion of PR man Adrian Wardour-Street. 'Ever noticed how girls bike along with one hand holding their skirts down? That's because, to be blunt, wind blows skirts up, reveals legs and causes traffic incidents. You know what beasts men are. I mean, well, OK, you can wear trousers or long heavy skirts or something really yuk like that, but glam-wise it's all a no-no.

'That's where one-wheeling is such a great thing. The pedals on a unicycle are directly below the saddle so a unicyclist reveals no more than a girl would when walking, right? That means we one-wheel girls can wear anything we like. And that means we can really get heavily into short skirts and leotards and short pants, to show as much as possible of those lovely legs I was telling readers how to get trim last week.'

But won't this cause even more pile-ups as men indulge in beastly ogling?

'Let it,' says Suzi. 'Who cares about men anyway? Stuff them, I say.'

But opposition to the growing unicycle trend is mounting among motorists. Defence of the Road, the motoring lobby determined to safeguard what it sees as a besieged position, has issued a statement blasting the unsafe presence of one-wheelers on the road, which it blames for three-quarters of Britain's road accidents. To check these figures I rang up the movement's head offices in Soho and talked to its head, Adrian Wardour-Street.

'Oh, hello, it's you again,' Adrian told me. 'Yes, this is just another little ploy we're trying to get unicycling on the map. We've always found that a little controversy does more to get things going than anything. Remember how skate-boarding really took off after it was banned from Hyde Park? It took me three months to persuade the GLC to do that. So I thought, well, it might be worth having a bash at raising the alarms over unicycling, as if it were a dangerous pastime. It is, actually. Only a loony would go out on the roads on one of those. You won't catch me doing it. But I confidently predict that one-wheeling will be a monster trend. Maybe not this afternoon. I have to knock off early. But tomorrow morning, definitely.'

Hair Today

'I view with deep suspicion any man who actually looks forward to going to the hairdresser, and does so more than once every three months.' *Beryl Downing, The Times.*

Well, I'm sorry, Beryl, but I absolutely *adore* going to the hairdresser. When my dynamic businesswoman wife wakes me up in the morning, which she does just as she leaves for work, and says 'Don't forget you're going to the hairdresser today' my heart leaps up, and so do I. Out of bed, into my Gucci pyjamas (I think one should dress for breakfast) and I simply tick off the minutes till it's time for the scissors, and shampoo, and those wonderful soothing fingertips again. I can hardly wait for my weekly visit to the hairdresser.

Weekly, I hear you say? A man who goes every week to the hairdresser? Well, I'm cheating just a teeny weeny bit there, because I actually go to three different hairdressers so I don't go into the same one more than once every three weeks. I always think, you see, that going to have your hair done is such fun that it's a crying shame to go to the same place each time. I mean, would one go to the same pub every time one felt thirsty? No, one wouldn't, would one. Well, there one is.

Hairdresser No 1 is a darling little place just off Bond Street called David and Vincent. Of course David isn't there any more because he had a flaming row with Vincent and absolutely flounced out, I can't tell you, to go and start his own place in St Albans. And then Vincent had a really terrible accident with his new roller skates (while actually cutting hair, would you believe) so now it's Michael and Humphrey, but they've kept the old name. Better, I say, than one of these silly names like Mr Scissors, or Sideburns.

Anyway, you arrive at David and Vincent and ask for your man, mine's Michael, and he says he'll be with you as soon as he's finished the new *Tatler*. Then one of his girls, I think she's a girl, wraps you in an Yves St Laurent blanket with armholes, for which you pay her £1, and another girl plunges your face in a basin and washes your hair (another £1) and throws you across the room into a chair. By now you feel wonderfully exhausted as if you'd been for a long swim, and it hasn't even started yet. Then Michael puts down his *Tatler* with a sigh (if he's not in it this month) and comes across to look at you.

This he does rather like a sculptor looks at a block of stone. You know, he stands behind you, arms folded, thinking to himself, My God, have we got to turn this into something looking like a human being? Then suddenly he comes to a decision and takes up his tools, or rather gets a boy, I think it's a boy, perhaps it hasn't made its mind up yet, to hand the tools to him. I could watch him at work for hours. In fact, I do watch him at work for hours. I think somewhere on the back of the seat there's one of those meters like they have in a taxi, just clocking up the time. Clip, snip, frown, turn my head, turn it back, sigh and start again. Honestly, I feel just like one of Toulouse-Lautrec's models.

He talks all the time, of course. About himself, of course. That's how I have come to know Michael's dreadful secret. He isn't gay. Apparently it's terribly difficult to get on in his line if you're not gay, and he had to pretend like mad when starting, but now he says he can easily pass. Soon he's thinking seriously about coming out and declaring that he's straight and he doesn't care who knows it, but he'll have to choose his moment.

Then come all the wonderful bottles full of things which he shakes over me, and then I open my wallet and shake money all over him, and a girl opens the door for me, which I tip her for, and it's only a week to go before I am due at my next hairdresser.

Of course, I don't need my hair cut by then, which is just as well, because at Jim's they don't do much haircutting. It's one of those Greek Cypriot places in the back of Soho down a staircase lined with photos of people who look as if they were failed film stars in 1956. The atmosphere is wonderful. Really masculine, and everything. You have to take your own coat off, and bring your own magazines, unless you enjoy the kind of weekly where the readers send in photos of their wives with no clothes on, and the radio has been on Radio 2 since 1940. What they do instead of cutting hair is dye people's moustaches, give them friction and shave them. Yes, really shave them, with soap and a blade and everything. But most of the time they do stitches, you know, friends of theirs come down bleeding rather a lot because they've been on the wrong end of a take-over bid in the dirty book trade, and hospitals would ask silly questions, so they come to the barber to be patched up. Marvellous. I, personally, just stay for a while and then buy a few contraceptives and go away again. I mean, fancy asking Michael for some. He'd go out of his mind. I don't use them myself, but I travel quite a lot in the Catholic Third World and they pay an absolute fortune for them out there, poor dears.

And then next week it's on to Jermyn Street for my visit to Clubb's, *the* hairdressers. By appointment, you know. My father put me down at birth as a member and I feel I owe it to the old boy. I don't really know what goes on at Clubb's. The scissors never actually meet your hair, just hover respectfully near it. Nobody says anything much. But the feel of the place is, I don't know, just like a cathedral - you know how when you go into a church and you don't actually believe a word of what's going on, but somehow that atmosphere of peace and tradition says something to you? Well, it's a lot like that at Clubb's. They've got one picture on the wall. It's of Gladstone. Most of the customers have the same haircut. He was bald when it was painted. When I come out of there I feel strangely uplifted. What I don't feel is as if I've had my hair cut, and I can see it's beginning to get a touch long not to mention where my sideburns are a shade too Mexican for comfort, but that doesn't really matter. After all, another seven days, and I'll be back in Michael's safe hands again. I just can't wait.

Sorry, Beryl.

Queen Mummery

(A TV studio. Bits of furniture made of glass and metal tubing, softened with leather. A vast staircase at the back. Down it comes Michael Parkinson. There is a huge ovation, as if there was something difficult about coming down a staircase. It dies away.)

Parkinson: Thank you. Tonight my guest is someone so wonderful and so truly magic that words fail me. How, you may ask, is that so different from normal? Let me just say that for everyone in this country this person has always been that bit more special than all the very special people who appear on my show. But without further ado, my guest tonight is – the Queen Mother!

(It is indeed the Queen Mother. What a catch for the *Parkinson Show*! How have they managed it? Does she think she is really appearing on *This Is Your Life*? Or getting a chance to meet Esther Rantzen? Whatever the reason, here she is, and down she comes. The crowd go wild. When she gets to the bottom of the stairs she waits as usual for a chair to be brought for her. At this point the producer would normally appear and say: 'Can we do that again and *this* time go over and sit with Mike?' That wouldn't seem quite right with the Queen Mum. Eventually Michael Parkinson brings a chair over and stands for the rest of the programme. The producer tears his hair out. It's very difficult getting one sitting, one standing person into a good camera shot.)

Parkinson: Your Majesty, this is a very proud moment for me. I spent a lot of time in the cinemas of Barnsley as a young lad and although like most young lads I fell in love with a different film star every week, I can truly say that my most abiding memory of those war years is of the star role you took, along with your husband George VI, in World War Two. And yet I believe I'm right in saying that, despite the wonderful performance you gave in World War Two, you hadn't been in showbiz very long.

Queen Mum: No.

Parkinson: If I'm right, your first big role came along in 1936. Your husband-and-wife act had been doing well, but not sensationally, and your roles as the Duke and Duchess of York had only been reviewed quietly. Then came your big chance. Edward VIII, the big West End smash hit of 1936, lost its leading pair and you were suddenly called upon to give the performance of a lifetime. That must have been a daunting moment.

Queen Mum: Yes.

Parkinson: Of course, there were really star performers in those days. Churchill, Roosevelt, Mussolini, Harold Larwood – I expect you met them all?

Queen Mum: Yes.

Parkinson: And I'm sure you have many a hilarious anecdote about those wonderful days when you, as Queen Elizabeth, were the quiet yet radiant star of a world that seems so far away to many of us who grew up in the next decade in the fleapits of Barnsley.

Queen Mum: Yes.

Parkinson: Good. Then came World War Two, and your never-to-be-forgotten performances – still as Queen Elizabeth – in a whole host of settings. On the balcony of Buckingham Palace, in hospitals, in the war zones. But above all we remember you for your appearances on location in the East End of London, playing the part of the mother of the nation who comes to comfort her people in times of trouble, for which of course you got your Academy Award. Troubled times. But I expect too there were many lighter moments among the bad times.

Queen Mum: Oh yes.

Parkinson: Such as the time when you found a little girl crying in the Whitechapel Road? And you asked her what the trouble was? And she said, she was crying because last night the German planes had knocked down the Duke of York? And you comforted her by saying that you were married to the Duke of York, and he was perfectly all right this morning? And she said, never mind yer 'usband, the Germans bombed the Duke of York last night and me dad was in the saloon bar?

Queen Mum: If you say so.

Parkinson: Now, of course, you're retired from showbiz, and for twenty years you haven't featured in a big production. There are many people who would like to see you make a comeback. But I suppose, for you, there must be a satisfaction in that one of your two children has gone on to be as big a star as you ever were. Though in some ways you must have had regrets that your other daughter, Margaret, never quite made the big time. Does it ever worry you that she has never been involved in a long-running success?

Queen Mum: Yes, and no.

Parkinson: Well, ma'am, it has been a real pleasure to have you on my show. I don't think we can let it end without a reference to the well-known fact that you like a bit of a sing-song. We have, in fact, a little bit of a surprise for you. (Enter Oscar Peterson, Stephane Grappelli, John Dankworth, Eric Morecambe, Rod Hull, Muhammad Ali, Fred Astaire, etc, all singing dancing and playing 'Happy Birthday to You'. Owing entirely to copyright difficulties over 'Happy Birthday', this show has not yet been put out on BBC-TV.)

A Life On The Ocean Bed

When I go sailing, I find it gives me plenty of time to think of answers to all those questions which puzzle me in life. Questions like, did I bring the boots that leak by mistake? Why is it always twenty degrees colder on a boat than on land 500 yards away? And, what the hell am I doing here?

Well, I know the answer to the last one immediately. I am here because my wife is nuts about sailing. As I sit in the cockpit, trying to work out in a rigorously scientific way if one foot really feels damper than the other, she is staring round, as keen as Columbus, to see if any ropes need tidying up, if the anchor chain is secured, whether the wind is changing its mind or if a boat a mile ahead will collide with us if we don't do something about it now. Legend has it that many a sailing man puts to sea with a not unwilling wife in tow. I am the only husband I know who follows in the wake of a salt water maniac.

Don't get me wrong (especially if you are my wife and happen to read this piece). I like sailing. I don't love it, but I like it. It's just that, for me, sailing tends to come into the category of sports which is headed by kite-flying. There are only two interesting moments in kite navigation; one is getting the kite off the ground and the other is getting it back down again. In between there is a long boring stretch which consists of you holding a piece of string in your hand and looking at a dot in the sky, with no apparent connection between the two. Flying kites is very closely followed by rowing. The Varsity Boat Race is without doubt the most boring sporting event invented by man. In fact, it is even more boring than kite-flying because it is only the start of the Boat Race which is interesting; within a few seconds it is obvious who is going to win, so the finish becomes boring as well.

Kite-flyers obviously realise the essentially boring nature of their sport, as they have introduced features to make it more interesting. In the East they have fighting kites with which they try to bring each other's kites down. Here in the West we have stunt kites on two strings which can dive and spiral and make interesting shapes with their long tails. I dare say, too, the Boat Race would be much more attractive if the rules were changed to allow the boats to ram each other and the crews board each other to engage in hand-to-hand grappling. As it is, the only Boat Races ever remembered are those in which one side has gratifyingly sunk.

But I will say this: sailing is much more interesting than rowing. I am not referring now to yacht racing, which is so full of rules and point-chasing that it is more like county cricket than anything. I am talking about sailing – getting in a boat and going somewhere. Anywhere. *Then* things start to happen. You look at the wind. You put up the right sails. The wind changes. You take down those sails and put up other sails. The wind

35

changes back. You put up the first sails again. The wind dies down. You switch on the engine. The engine does not work. You anchor and have lunch. The wind springs up again and the boat tips. The lunch falls on the cockpit floor. There is never a dull moment. Hardly.

Last weekend my wife and I went on a friend's boat to sail up the Suffolk coast from Burnham, for a week. This I looked forward to, as we were going to many places I had never seen. (Would the Boat Race not also be improved, by the way, if the rowers had to get out at every pub they passed and have a quick pint?) And on the very first day we visited a place that none of us had dreamt we would ever visit. The Maplin Sands.

Quite how it happened is still open to dispute, but I am glad to say that it was my wife at the helm and the captain navigating when it happened. I was sitting in the cockpit, busy with my boot problem. What happened was, in landlubber's terms, that we steered a bit to one side, hit the hard shoulder and stayed there. The keel dug a hole for itself in the hidden sands and stuck. We tried everything we knew. We switched on the engine. The battery was flat. We went to look for the

36

starting handle. It wasn't there. We found it somewhere else. It was too late to try the engine by then. We cursed. We swore. That didn't work either.

After a quarter of an hour we suddenly became resigned to the fact that we were going to be there for twelve hours (six for the tide to go down, six for it to come up and take us off) and from that moment the whole thing became immensely enjoyable. As the boat settled further and further on its side we discovered the delights of walking round the walls of a room (remember Fred Astaire dancing on the ceiling?). The water suddenly became only an inch deep and we could get off and walk around in the sea. Equally suddenly we were on miles and miles of wet but firm sand and could go for long walks away out to sea. Sea birds, the only inhabitants, came to study this new kind of protected wild life. The two children on board discovered stranded jelly fish and set up impromptu biology classes. The captain announced that it was customary on these occasions to drink more red wine than was good for you, so we climbed into the tiny dinghy towed behind and had the most enormous lunch followed by the most enormous siesta. At about tea-time we even had a caller; a boat anchored nearby and the crew came over in a dinghy to see if we were all right. We gave him a biscuit and he went away.

And soon but gradually the sun went down over this vast expanse of whispering sand, and tip-toeing waves, and the moon, a great big orange boiled sweet, floated up out of the distant land. The water began to return. It floated the dinghy. Then it started to right the boat so that, having only just learnt to ignore the floors and walk on the sticking out edges of seats or on the bookshelf, we had to remember all over again about the right-way-up world. Came ten o'clock, and under the bright moonlight we started the engine sweetly first time and smoothly slid back into the right channels.

The rest of the week was fine. We sailed up and down rivers, tackled choppy weather off Harwich and caught the right tides entering the Deben, avoiding skilfully much more tricky sands than Maplin. I enjoyed it. I really did. Especially as by then I had discovered that my boots were the watertight ones. But the funny thing is that, when I look back, the day that stands out for me is the day we spent on the Maplin Sands, the day we didn't do any sailing at all, when a whole new world opened up.

I'm not sure what the moral is. Except, perhaps, that apart from all the other improvements I've mentioned, the Boat Race would be much more exciting if staged at the lowest point of the tide on a part of the Thames where there was only room for one boat to get through without going aground.

Kington's Book of Lists

Ten Misleading Remarks Heard in Everyday Conversation.
'Things are fine, thanks.'
'... and it's the only drink I know which never gives you a hangover.'
'I don't think it's actually going to rain.'
'I know you're going to like him.'
'We only watch when there's something really good on.'
'We must keep in touch.'
'Gosh, no, I'm not very good at the game at all.'
'I have nothing against him personally, but ...'
'Apparently it has aphrodisiac qualities.'
'I'll just come in for coffee, then.'

Ten Most Read Magazines in Britain
Caravan and Yacht Owner
Motorbike and Caravan Owner
Yacht and Penthouse Owner
Yachtmen Only
Skate, Bike and Yacht Monthly
Skaters' Digest
The Times Boating Supplement
The Incredible Hulk Meets Yachtsman
Ms Yachtperson

Ten Objects Rarely Found in the Average Household
String

Spare can-opener
Fuses
Unused stamps
The newspaper with that article you were going to cut out
A pencil within twenty feet of the telephone
Parsley
The drink your guest asks for
An umbrella

Ten Very Common Objects in the Average Household
Dead parsley
An empty ice tray
Last week's *Time Out*
A phone number on a piece of paper, with no name
A match box, with one match in it, dead
A screw lying on the floor, without any apparent origin
Gin but not tonic, or tonic, but not gin
A pile of records and empty sleeves; ten records, nine sleeves
A pair of underpants disclaimed by all residents
A tube of toothpaste, started yesterday, almost empty today

Ten Extremely Annoying Sounds
The sniffing of a human being
The singing of a sparrow
The raving of a motor bike radio
The chimes of an ice cream van
The clapping of a rock audience recognising a tune
The singing at the Last Prom
The poetry voices on Radio 3
The noises in the empty flat upstairs
The ringing of a phone after bedtime
The sound of brown envelopes coming through the letter box

Ten Very Boring Conversationalists
Jazz enthusiasts
Motorists with good short cuts
People who are reminded of stories
Those who do not own TV sets or cars
People who have just given up something
People who have just been burgled

People who can still remember their dreams in detail

Those who would rather talk about wine than drink it

People who have seen a good film or programme that you haven't

People who tell long boring stories about events that happened to you and them twenty years ago (inevitably parents or spouses)

Ten Absolutely Vital Things to know about Taking a Bath

Spiders can run round baths faster than you can.

When you leave a bath to run by itself, the plug jumps out just as you leave the bathroom, and you return to an empty bath just as the hot water runs out.

If you run a bath too hot and then add some cold water, the cold water stays at the tap end. You never realise this until you sit in the other end and burn your bottom.

When you lie back in a bath, your right foot slides forward until it is positioned exactly beneath the dripping tap.

It is physically impossible to turn a tap on or off with your foot.

Lost soap is always behind you.

The odd flannel you are using to wash yourself is not a flannel at all; it is a sock which has just fallen from the clothes line above.

The dirt which you wash off yourself gathers on the surface of the water and then reattaches itself to you as you rise to leave.

When you get out of the bath, the first bit you dry is the one bit you suddenly realise you forgot to wash.

However hard you dry yourself, you are still wet when you put your clothes on.

Christmas Notions

Most of us solve some of our Christmas gift problems by

saving up those unwanted presents from last year and giving them away this year. It's very important, of course, to remember who they were from, so that you don't give them back to the actual person who gave them to you – and *do* remember to take off that incriminating label saying 'Love From Granny'. Unless of course you are Granny.

Other presents can, with a little thought, be entirely free. One amusing idea is to give posters. Not the glittering Police and Ian Dury posters which cost so much at your local record store, but the huge hoardings which stand guard over our roundabouts. Did you know that big firms are only too glad to give away posters measuring more than ten by twenty feet? Ideal if you know a young couple who haven't wallpapered their room yet. Also, at this time of the year there are a lot of 1980 A–D phone books standing around unclaimed at the bottom of blocks of flats. Do you have a friend who fancies his strength? Send him one labelled 'Try tearing this in half!'. Or it would make interesting wallpaper for young couples who are tired of having huge posters on the wall.

I was talking to a street cleaner the other day, and he tells me that his work sweeping leaves into black plastic bags is somewhat relieved by all the gardeners who beg him for a few sacks for their compost heaps. We all have friends and parents who are bitten by the gardening bug – why not give them leaves this year? Put a little sticker on each bag saying 'Organically Grown English Leaves from Real Trees'. Or could make an unusual wallpaper.

Children, of course, are a problem. You give them a train set or their own Space Invaders machine, and within minutes it's broken down, and they're playing with what they really like – a bit of string, two sticks, an old toilet roll and an empty yoghurt pot. So give them exactly that: in a large plain box, marked £5.95, 'An Educational Toy from the *Guardian* Women's Page'.

Sooner or later, though, you'll have to splash out money on presents by actually going into shops and buying something. Here are this year's ideas.

Wrapping Paper It's getting desperately expensive just to wrap presents these days so why not *give* wrapping paper? Only £3 a sheet from Fruit of the Tree, Kings Road.

Guitar Strings Everyone knows someone who plays the

guitar i.e. owns a guitar which he hasn't touched for years. Guitar strings are surprisingly cheap and the recipient will never admit that he has forgotten all his positions.

Candles There's something nice about candles, isn't there? Useless, but nice. On sale at all good Roman Catholic churches.

A Can of Coca-Cola Coke tins turn up in all sort of guises these days – as transistor radios, as cigarette lighters, handkerchief containers, string dispenser ... but nobody ever gets the real thing for Christmas. Might look better if labelled 'A present from the Tate Gallery'.

Emergency Household Kit Make a list of the ten things most liable to be missing just when you need them – a light bulb, fuse wire, a lemon, pencil and paper near the telephone, box of matches, etc. Buy them all and put them in a gift box. To allay any objections, label 'Made in the Third World'.

Christmas Boxes The one thing we all forget till the last moment – tips for the dustman, postman, etc. Do it for someone else! Just give them a bundle of envelopes marked For The Milkman, For the Carol Singers, etc. Up to you what you put in them.

Gyles Brandreth's Bumper Book of Edwardian Country Lady Jokes This year's Christmas best-seller. Or was it last year? Anyway, as it's happily remaindered, you should pick it up for less than 50p.

Grow-Your-Own Oak Tree Kit Yes, all you need to have your own mighty monarch of the forest! An acorn in an envelope.

Unmatching Sock Set The ultimate Christmas present. Who wants matching sock sets, when the greatest problem in household laundry is the accumulating amount of socks that seem to have no mate? Either snap up the incredibly cheap single sock offers at all good railway lost property offices, or collect your own from the back of your drawers.

Thank You Letters

To the milkman

Dear milkman, how can I ever say thank you for all the pints of gold top, red top, and stripey top you have left me this year, when all I ever asked for was silver top? The single cream at times when I needed double? And that unforgettable day when I put in a special order of single cream and you left six pineapple yoghurts? Dear milkman, I wish you could have tasted the potatoes-in-cream dish I made all unsuspectingly from those six pineapple yoghurts. Dear, dear milkman, I know you will understand when you find that the fiver you expected me to leave for you this Christmas is instead a 50p piece. In your own words, the order you wished was not to hand.

To the Reader's Digest

I was stunned by your present. Why, we hardly know each other, yet I have been selected from so many million to enter your free contest in which I may win £25,000. I have already spent three hours poring over the entry form, and I think I can honestly say I am beginning to see how it should be filled in. The best bit of the present, of course, was where you say that I do not have to buy a subscription to *Reader's Digest*. Can this really be true? No one has ever said that to me before. You have made me very happy.

Dear 24-Hour Plumber

Your offer to clear my blocked drains at any hour of day or night came right out of the blue on one of those days when I hadn't received any Christmas cards or friendly letters, know what I mean? It really cheered me up. In fact, the only other mail I had that day was from a man offering to clear my furniture any hour of day or night, a man offering to take me anywhere by minicab (day or night) and from a new restaurant offering to feed me at any time, except Sundays. I personally do not need any drains cleared, but I am forwarding the addresses of the minicab man, restaurant and furniture clearer to you in case they do. I have also, of course, forwarded your address to them. I hope you will hear from them.

To HM Government
I am very grateful for the timely warning you printed on the packet of cigarettes I bought this morning. I had no idea. I immediately threw them away. But you may also be interested to learn that cigarettes, in addition, leave burn marks, make rooms smell nasty, ruin the flavour of kisses, cause ash on floors and taste pretty foul. Any chance of warning people about that?

To the local council
I should have written long ago to thank you for the skip you occasionally leave on our corner marked AMENITY RUB-BISH. As it is always full half an hour after you leave it (perhaps you leave it full to start with?), I have never had occasion to use it, but I appreciate the thought. Especially as our dustmen never take away anything larger than an empty tissue box. At this moment I have a small broken-down pram I am trying to get rid of, and have often thought of hailing a passing totter. However, there are no passing totters. Perhaps they too now leave skips on street corners for the public to fill. So you can imagine that I have been driven quite desperate trying to think of a way of getting rid of it.

I have now thought of a neat compromise. *You* can have the pram as a Christmas present. Rather than stuff it in an already crammed AMENITY RUBBISH dump, I will leave it on the Town Hall steps next week. I *know* you will find a good use for it.

To the makers of Saratoga Shirts
The other day I bought one of your shirts. It was a good shirt. It did all the things that shirts are meant to do. It covered my torso and hung down behind when I thought it was tucked in. But imagine my confusion when I found all the free gifts you had included with the shirt! To wit, one cellophane bag, one cardboard collar shape, four plastic clips, two metal paper clips, one long blue thread, one internal cardboard skeleton,

44

seven sharp pins which I extracted and one which I didn't. Thank you for your intense generosity. I have converted them into a model of the Eiffel Tower.

To the Sunrise Club, Romford
Thank you for pressing into my hand an invitation to your club. Thank you for saying that if I come at 6.30 on a Monday I will get in free. Thank you for offering one complimentary glass of white wine. Thank you for letting me bring a girlfriend at no extra charge. I hope you will not be offended if I stay home and watch television. You may come and watch too, if you arrive before 6.30 and bring a girl. There will be one glass of plonk going.

To the editor of The Times
Many thanks for your wonderful free supplement on 'Problems in Korean Development' which fell out of your paper this

morning. It made a nice light-hearted alternative to Bernard Levin.

Sure You're In The Right Job?

Melanie, 29, Temp Company Director
'It's not just secretaries who go on holiday and have to be temporarily replaced, you know. Executives go on holiday as well. More, probably. Anyway, I fill in for them. If a director's away for four weeks, I go round and do his normal functions – having lunch with people, going to meetings, popping up to the Birmingham branch, that sort of thing. People like to know that things are going on as normal. Of course, I don't take things too seriously; if I started turning up on time every day and getting through lots of letters, that would make the bloke who's away look very bad, so I just sort of drift through the day. I don't make any big decisions unless I'm very bored; the last firm I was with, I was so fed up by the last week that I changed their whole marketing operation in the Middle East. It worked so well that they've offered me a directorship, but I don't really want to be tied down to a job yet.'

Lucy, 24, Model
'I model for a tattooist. Well, I mean, a tattooist has got to have models like any artist, hasn't he? It's not all out of his head, is it? Being a mermaid is the easiest. In the morning I pose topless, in the afternoon I hold up a big cod for the tail. In the evening we have a big fry-up. The hardest is posing for blokes who want a bowsprit and figurehead on their chest. Ever tried posing for two hours leaning over at 45°? Well, then.'

Denise, 26, Shoplifter
'I'm employed by a big Oxford Street store to shoplift.

Sounds funny, doesn't it? But the way they see it, if shoppers see a shoplifter being arrested, it discourages a lot of them from doing the same. Well, you can't guarantee detectives spotting real shoplifters, so they've hired me to pose as one. I get arrested, oh, seven or eight times a day. I'm getting good at it now. Bit of screaming, or a bit of crying, or even throw a complete tantrum, then off to the manager's office. Off to the make-up section to do my face again, then back on duty. The detectives aren't too hot, actually, and sometimes I get clean out of the shop without being stopped. Got some lovely stuff at home, now. Still, it's all perks isn't it?'

Rosie, 25, Bill-Sticker
'I did two years at polytechnic, then three years at the Royal College of Art, and now I'm into posters in a big way. Sticking them up on shop windows, I mean. Ever wondered who pastes those fly posters up on empty shops? A lot of us are up and about at dawn, doing it. It's part of urban art, the way I see it. An empty shop, to me, is like a canvas just waiting to be given form and colour. Fancy getting paid to do it as well!'

Gerry, 29, First Division Goalkeeper
'Up until my sex change operation last year, I was goalkeeper with a big London team. Still am, actually. The rest of the lads don't know about it. It hasn't affected my goalkeeping, but it's affected my attitude to my goal, which is definitely the neatest and best kept in London. Some goalies just don't seem to care how scruffy or badly looked after the goals are, honestly, you'd think they had no pride. I'm thinking of putting flowers in now, but I don't know; it might look a bit odd. What do you think?'

Sheila, 32, Spy
'Of course, Sheila isn't my right name. Being a spy, I couldn't tell you my real name. And 32 isn't my right age. When you're a spy you have to be so careful. To give you some idea, I can tell you that I'm not actually a spy at all – I'm a go-go dancer in a West End club. I couldn't possibly tell you which club. I mean, when you're a go-go dancer, you've got to be *really* careful.'

Susie, 25, Roller Skater

'I'm employed by the GLC Parks Department to brighten up the parks. You don't think all those trendy figures on skates are private individuals, do you? Half of them are laid on by the GLC to give the parks a bit of je ne sais quoi. Last year I was a skate-boarder, year before a jogger. Ever so decorative, you know. Bit harder this year, because I can't really get the hang of these earphones. Especially when you're listening to the new Police single and a voice suddenly breaks in: 'Park skaters, park skaters, go immediately to St James's for early lunch crowd.' It's getting a bit hard on the ankles, too. I've applied for a transfer to the kite-flying section.'

Felicity, 34, Resting Actress

'Push off, mate. I'm trying to get some rest.'

What Ever Happened To Covent Garden?

The Skipping Rope Shop

Here you can find almost every kind of skipping rope known to man. Did you know that in Thailand they have fighting skipping ropes up to ten feet long? Or that in parts of Africa a man's status is judged by the number of beads on his skipping rope? Not very interesting, is it? The Skipping Rope Shop isn't doing very well.

Après-Blitz

The wine bar for last year's beautiful people, those unfortunate wretches who were at the crest of the wave in about October but who now, at over twenty-one, are beginning to slide over the top. They meet at lunch and every evening to reminisce about 1980 and to wonder if it'll ever be worth getting their skates out again.

The Opera Bike Shop
Basically the Bike Shop are into bikes as a viable meaningful *ecological* unit in city life, and also as a good way of getting around. But they preserve all the traditional facets of the old-style bike shop: e.g. the customer in front of you engaged in an endless discussion about something he's not even going to buy, the shop being crammed with unopened cases, the bikeman answering the phone just when it's your turn to be served, the thing you want not being in stock and you being convinced it's in one of those cases. The atmosphere is terribly friendly.

Paddington's
An all-evening hamburger and wine place run by Roger Paddington. 'Basically,' he says, 'this is the restaurant that I have always dreamed of running, i.e. somewhere where beautiful young girls are prepared to work cheaply as waitresses and feel unable to resist my advances.' Very quick turnover of food, customers and staff. Some customers stay longer than the girls.

Gay Blades
The most advanced hair cuttery in London from the unisex angle; when customers leave, it's impossible to tell if they're men or women.

Krud
The ultimate joke shop. Almost all of their merchandise is in such bad taste, or so offensive or even explosive, that very little of it is on display. 'We do mostly mail order,' says genial jokey owner Ted Wilt, 'and, boy, do our customers get a surprise when they open their mail orders. We're sort of like the IRA in light-hearted mood.'

Superveg
Probably the most expensive greengrocer in London, Superveg's assistants dress in top hat, white tie and tails to serve you the mushrooms at £1 a quarter. £1 may seem a lot for only a quarter of a mushroom, but you really feel you've had an experience.

Turnover

A boutique stocked entirely with stuff shoplifted from other shops in Covent Garden. Amazing variety of goods. They have some problems with pilferage; close-circuit TV cameras were installed at Christmas but someone nicked them.

Third World Gift Shop

This actually started out as a place where the public could leave gifts for the Third World, but so many inquiries were received for Peruvian ponchos and Cambodian wicker things that they started selling instead.

La Petit Café Français Terriblement Authentique

The food and wine at this little bistro is more or less the same as at any other imitation French restaurant (paté, quiche, mussels) but the waiters are flown in fresh from Paris every day, thus guaranteeing their authenticity, cheekiness, arrogance, superciliousness and inability to speak English or much French either come to that. They all leave the next day to start their own bistros.

The Limb Shop

Beautiful preparations in beautiful packaging at beautiful prices. One hardly dares to use them. I bought a pot of Cucumber Conditioner two weeks ago and still haven't opened it. To be honest, I don't quite see the point of conditioning cucumbers. But it looks good in the kitchen.

Trublove, Greenhouse and Parkbench

The most wonderful jams, chutneys and preserves. Well, the jams themselves aren't much, but the jars and pots are terrific and the labels out of this world. This is because the preserves aren't for eating - they're for giving as presents.

Mr Topper

The ultimate in smart Covent Garden shops. Wood panelling. Lovely old wood floors. Cut glass windows. Vases of flowers. Lovely chairs for the customer to sit in. And - here's the crunch - Mr Topper doesn't sell anything. 'I always wanted to open my own shop,' says Mr Topper - real name Earl of Newport Pagnell - 'but never wanted to get involved with buying and selling. People come in here not to get sordid objects and hand over plastic cash cards; they come here to get away from all that. This is just, simply, a very, very, *nice* shop.'

The Big, Bad, City

In the control room of the Police Missing Persons Department stands a giant computer. One glance at its dials will tell you exactly how many people are missing in England today, not counting 10,000 Chelsea supporters lost since 1977. It won't tell you where they are, why they have gone or whether they would come back if only Dad switched that damned TV off, but it knows exactly how many there are. As Sergeant Whifforth glanced at the display unit, he noted that the fingers stood at 29,002. Same height as Everest, he thought. Assuming they're all lying down, of course. Then, as he watched, the figure changed to 29,003.

'Some other poor devil gone missing,' he said out loud.

Shirley Stevens was the 29,003rd missing person. At that very moment she was stepping across the threshold of her parents' home in some dreadful northern town - let us call it Bradford - clutching her suitcase and a single ticket to London.

'Hallo, Shirl,' said her father up a ladder doing the hedge. 'Running away from home, then?'

'Yes,' said Shirley resolutely. 'I can't stand it any more. The same dreary meals. The awful people. The perpetual little tawdry dramas enacted day after day.'

'I don't like "Crossroads" much meself,' said father. 'You can always switch over, tha knowest.'

'You don't understand!' said Shirley. 'I'm going to the big city!'

'Leeds?' said Dad. 'What's so special about Leeds?'

This conversation might have gone on all day till father ran

51

out of folksy backchat, had not Shirley proudly tossed her locks and walked off down the road towards the station. God, her parents were so narrow! They thought she was still a little girl, an irresponsible layabout. They had no understanding of her ambition to go to London, meet Adam Ant, get his autograph and fall in with a pathetic crowd of pill-poppers in Piccadilly Circus, then creep home about six months later half-starved. She tossed her locks proudly again. She was very good at tossing her locks proudly, as you would be if you had practised in front of a mirror for three years. Besides, having subjected her locks to a tough treatment of chemicals over three years, ranging from henna to peroxide through mango chutney, she knew that she might have no hair left at twenty and felt she ought to toss her locks while she had some.

On Bradford station she met a familiar figure. It was her mother.

'Dad told me as how you were running away from home. We were both of us heart-broken. We've scrimped and saved since tha were a tiny lass to get thee a decent hair-cut. But 'twere to no avail. Howsomever, since th'art leaving home, we felt tha ought to have this.'

Shirley looked down. It was a copy of *Talk Yorkshire and Impress People Down South*.

'Oh, mother,' said Shirley. 'For heaven's sake, grow up! People don't talk like that any more, you silly old bean.'

Mother gazed at her helplessly for a moment, then clouted her with her Yorkshire dictionary before striding proudly from the station. Feeling on the verge of tears, Shirley staggered to the train and collapsed in the first class seat facing the engine she had reserved weeks before.

The train was full of proud Yorkshire lasses going to the big city to become top dress designers, opening bats for England or just members of The Police Fan Club. Meanwhile, their first ambition was to get a tea and packet of biscuits in the buffet bar. At least, Shirley's was.

There was a shriek of girlish laughter from the other women in the buffet bar, all of whom had brought a thermos flask of Newcastle Brown and a packet of cold Yorkshire pudding, plus a D H Lawrence paperback, to while away the long journey.

'What have we got here?' laughed their leader, brave Bridget
Batkin of the Upper VI at St Pancras School for Girls. 'I say,
you girls, do you think we ought to tell this funny little
creature what she can expect in London?'

'Rather!' came the cry.

'Right ho, chaps,' said Bridget, giving Shirley's ear a
friendly tweak. Shirley could have cheerfully brained her, and
in fact was fated to do so three years later at a party given by
the last Earl of Swinfield. But that is another story.

'Look here, little thing,' said Bridget, 'London isn't like
Bradford. For one thing, people there aren't half so warm and

friendly. On the other hand, they've got a damned sight more money.'

Cheers interrupted her peroration. Shirley, who had no idea what a peroration was, kept quiet.

'And thirdly, you are bound to meet a man on the platform of your London terminus who will try to tempt you into the most degrading way of life. My advice is ...' She looked around at the circle of enrapt faces ... '... say yes!'

The girls all cheered like mad. Never! thought Shirley ...

Despite herself, Shirley looked round at St Pancras for the villain who would make her life a misery. She knew what he would look like. Swarthy, tall, with dark eyes, wearing the wrong-coloured tie and having a luggage trolley ready. There were many there like that. None of them approached her.

'Excuse me,' said a gentle voice. 'You look as if you're having the most awful trouble with that luggage.'

Shirley looked up into a beige pair of eyes, as trustworthy as an old school blazer, and fell in love immediately.

'Fact is,' he said, 'we're looking for someone fresh in our copyright department, and you look just the sort of gal we need.'

Father looked up troubled from her first letter home.

'Ah'm worried about our Shirley,' he said. 'I had hoped she would get stuck in as a nice high class call-girl or summat, but here she is tarting around in publishing. Doing this and that for any author that happens to come along. I hope she knows what she's doing.'

Sergeant Whifforth briefly glanced up from the computer. 'We can delete 29,003 from the reckoning,' he said. 'She's gone into publishing. There's no hope for her.'

Lessons That Life Has Taught Me

The only maths master I ever remember having was a man called J F K Melluish. There must have been others. I mean, somebody must have shown me the way from 1 to 9, and then demonstrated that if you put two of these numbers together you got a bigger number – it's like a glorified and intellectual form of sex education – but I don't know who and I still don't really see why it works. Just because 6 times 9 has always equalled 54 never seems to me quite good enough a reason for supposing it will do so next week, and if it does, then it seems too predictable to me to be worth bothering about.

Mr Melluish was different. Not that the maths he taught was any different. It was just worse. We went on to trigonometry with him. I never understood how trigonometry worked – all I can remember is that I was the first person in the class to be able to spell it properly, which should have given me the clue that I was better at writing than figuring. The same applied when Mr Melluish said: 'If four men take four hours to dig a trench, how long will it take thirteen men ...' I wasn't interested in the mathematical answer, only in these four men digging the trench, and how patiently they'd worked, when along come these nine other men to finish the job, and how choked these four men would be. 'Will the four men work slower because they're fed up with not being trusted?' I'd ask Mr Melluish. 'And isn't it unlucky for thirteen men to dig a trench? And anyway, wouldn't they all get in each other's way?' 'Shut up,' he'd explain helpfully.

No, what made Mr Melluish different was that one day he suddenly deserted maths and said he was about to say something very important, something more important than anything he'd taught us before.

We all perked up. Maybe this was the long-awaited embarrassing sex education bit. (It wasn't. To this day the only talk

55

I've had on sex was from an embarrassed headmaster about the reproduction of lupins. I'm as ready as can be if I ever fall in love with a lupin.) Instead, he said that at all times in life we should have the following emergency items about our person.

1   A piece of string.
2   A piece of paper and a stamp.
3   A pen-knife.
4   A shilling.

It sounds simple, but it's wonderful advice – great advice. I've never needed to use trigonometry, but often I have had cause to thank Mr Melluish that I have a string to replace shoe-laces or tie up trousers with, and a pen-knife to do everything else with. Trigonometry is all very well, is my message to Bertrand Russell, but it doesn't keep your trousers up.

However, in the twenty years since Mr Melluish dragged me kicking and yawning through Maths 'O' Level, a great deal of water has passed under the bridge (480 gallons per hour, actually, which makes ...) and three things have happened to me: inflation, maturity and some very painful chilblains in 1963. Drawing on these experiences I would now expand and change the Melluish list to read as follows.

1   A pound note and five 10p coins. The pound is to buy yourself a half of bitter in extremes and the 10p coins are to put in slot machines such as one-armed bandits or phone boxes (the odds on both are about the same, incidentally).
2   A roll of lavatory paper. This is something I picked up in South America. Not only are most lavatories devoid of paper, but they use their roll for many other things as well – wiping faces, staunching wounds, taking down addresses, wedging under table legs, making ear plugs from. It replaces Mr Melluish's piece of paper.
3   A corkscrew. Best is the so-called waiter's friend, which is a combined corkscrew and knife blade. I suppose it says something about me that I need the corkscrew more often. But corkscrews can be used for other things beside screwing corks. I once sprang to the rescue of a yacht owner who had lost his shackle key, by operating on his mast as if it were a bottle of Nuits St Georges. Corkscrews are very good for clearing plug-holes after every thousandth shampoo. And I was once stranded on the A40 at night in a friend's car because he had a puncture and hadn't got a screwdriver to get the hub cap off

56

with. Did you know you can get a hub cap off with a corkscrew? Not immediately, maybe, but eventually.

4   A pin. I can never remember what the pin is for, but people keep asking me for it, so it must be useful for something. The only thing I've ever used a pin for is pricking a blister, and first you have to sterilise it, for which you need …

5   A box of matches. Or maybe a book of matches. A book is better, because it's free and also because it gives the police something to work on when they find your corpse. It's not much fun for them if the only clue they've got is a box of matches. 'All we've got to do is check all Bryant and May's customers in the last couple of weeks,' they say despondently. Much better if you have a book of matches marked Ronnie Scott's Club. I've got one. Haven't been there for months, but you can't make it too easy for them.

6   The measurements of your loved one. There's nothing worse than buying some flash underwear or wonderful local garment as a last-minute present and then not knowing what size to buy.

7   A credit card. Gets Yale locks open in a jiffy.

8   Photographs of your children. It's amazing how foreigners soften up on the production of these. If you haven't got any photos – or any children – borrow some. All children look alike to foreigners.

9   An empty polythene bag. If you've got it, you'll never need it, but – and this is what life's all about, children – if you haven't got one, you'll need one desperately.

10   A pencil. Miles better than a pen, which you can't sharpen, and pencil writing doesn't run in the rain, nor can you clear out ear wax with a pen.

11   A bottle of pickled onions. That's for those nasty chilblains I got in 1963. You heat the juice as hot as you can bear it, and dab it on. Works wonders. No, of course I don't carry a jar of pickled onions round with me. Come to that, I don't carry most of these things round with me. I'm just telling you what experience has taught me. Experience comes from being caught unprepared, not being caught prepared.

Chemical Warfare

(In the longest trial in pharmaceutical history, Lord Howard de Pilatory, current chairman of Grotty Body Products, is facing 13,450 charges of deceiving the public. He pleads not guilty to all of them. This is an extract from day 43).

Counsel: I have here another of your products, a tin marked Cucumber Skin Conditioner. Would you please tell the court what effect this product has?

Defendant: Certainly. When rubbed on, it makes the skin of a cucumber exceptionally supple and lustrous.

Counsel: What effect does it have on the human skin?

Defendant: It makes it green.

Counsel: Do you not think the public is being deceived?

Defendant: Not at all. It is very fashionable to be green.

Counsel: Hmm. I have here another product, a shampoo called Milkmaid Cream. On the label it says in large letters NEW! IMPROVED! Now, laboratory tests show that it is no way different from your previous shampoo called Milkmaid Cream. Can you tell us what is new and improved?

Defendant: Certainly. The lettering is new and improved. It is twice as large as before. Also, we are using a totally new picture of a milkmaid which is much more attractive than the previous one.

Counsel: Are you suggesting that the change of a label can change the product?

Defendant: I would go further than that. It is the *only* thing that can change a product. We spend hundreds of thousands of pounds on the design of labels and packagings.

Counsel: With what result?

Defendant: We have to increase the price of the product. But that, of course, also improves it.

Counsel: How?

Defendant: It is well-known that you only get what you pay for. Therefore, the more you pay, the better you get.

Counsel: I see. I have here another bottle of shampoo, marked 'Greasy Shampoo, for Lemony Hair!' Are you seriously suggesting that people suffer from lemony hair?

Defendant: Of course. They use too much lemon shampoo. Greasy Shampoo restores the natural oils. It also makes a good salad dressing.

Counsel: Well, that is as it may be. Now, here I have a jar made by you marked Skin Reconditioner. Could you explain what this means?

Defendant: Glad to. In the ordinary face-care session, a girl will wash her face, apply cleanser, add moisturiser, use pre-conditioner, put on cream and then apply make-up. As a result of this treatment her skin is absolutely exhausted. Hence the need for Skin Reconditioner.

Counsel: What is the result?

Defendant: Her skin falls off, but not for years yet. Meanwhile it makes her look extremely alluring and leads to romantic attachments.

Counsel: How can you be sure?

Defendant: We have tested the product.

Counsel: On young girls?

Defendant: No. On rats.

Counsel: With what result?

Defendant: In every case, we have enabled young, lonely rats to develop strong and enduring relationships. Also, they go out dancing a lot.

Counsel: With other rats?

Defendant: Well, no. With empty bottles of Skin Reconditioner, actually. But the general effect has been good.

Counsel: I would like to put it to you that you are marketing at great expense products which have little or no effect on the customer.

Defendant: Of course. That is what beauty care is all about.

Counsel: What have you to say about Honey and Camomile Tea?

Defendant: That's very kind – I'd love a cup.

Counsel: I really meant, how do you justify your marketing of this product? Your slogans say 'Look good enough for a Royal Wedding – drink Honey 'n' Camomile Tea!' Are you suggesting that this tea will make you like Lady Diana Spencer?

59

Defendant: No. Like Prince Charles.

Counsel: How?

Defendant: It makes your ears stick out.

Counsel: How exactly?

Defendant: You stick a cube behind each ear.

Counsel: I see. You also market a kind of soap called Orange and Oatmeal. What advantage can there be in mixing orange with oatmeal?

Defendant: It makes your porridge an interesting colour, I suppose.

Counsel: I meant, in a soap?

Defendant: Ah, well. At the moment there is a great vogue for mixing two flavours in everything. Yoghurts, for instance, are all Apricot 'n' Melon; ice creams are Rum 'n' Chocolate ... we are merely following public taste.

Counsel: That's interesting. So that's the reason, is it?

Defendant: No. The *real* reason is that most girls are trying to slim. So they are always feeling hungry. So the more foods we mention on our beauty products, the more likely they are to buy them. *But they don't actually eat them.* So our shampoos are, really, a slimming aid.

Counsel: Is that why you market a Mushroom 'n' Tomato Shampoo?

Defendant: Not really. It's a failed ketchup we bought cheap and relabelled.

Counsel: And does it work?

Defendant: Well, our rats love it. Also, most of them have developed long soft silky hair.

Counsel: What is so good about soft, silky hair?

Defendant: If you had it, you wouldn't ask. But I cannot help noticing that you are bald.

Counsel: There is nothing I can do about that.

Defendant: Not so fast! Have you tried our Oyster 'n' Bacon Hair Restorer?

Counsel: No, but it sounds nice.

Defendant: Of course it does! All our products sound nice to the people they are aimed at. That is why it is foolish to accuse me of deceiving the public. The public *wants* to be deceived. Here – take a sachet of our Smoked Salmon Shampoo. Makes lawyer's wigs look even more distinguished.

Counsel: Gee, thanks.

60

Defendant: Be my guest. (*The trial continues*)

North V T'South

Never mind about Russia and Poland – has anyone noticed that the North is poised for an invasion of the South? Put it another way; has anyone noticed that the North has *already* invaded the South? And that the tanks have already rolled into London? The tanks in this case are full of beer, Northern beer, rolling down the M1 and discharging their poison gases into our southern pubs.

You must have seen the ads. Wilson's Beer from Manchester. John Smith's Ale from Somewhere-on-Trent. Samuel Smith's Right Powerful Brew from Yorkshire. You have to be called Smith or Wilson or summat down to earth to brew beer in the North, that's the message, and you have to be a real man or a right lass to drink the stuff. Get it down, you, lad – it'll put hair on your vest, damp stains on your trousers and a lot of money in the northern economy. Happen it will keep you out at the pub all evening, which doesn't do much for a marriage down south, maybe, but up north that sort of thing cements a relationship even more than getting up at four am to go fishing.

It's happening in food as well. Have you seen the ads for faggots? Well, *have* you seen the ads for faggots? Of course you've seen the ads for bloody faggots! You've probably even gone and been and bought some. And eaten them with mushy peas. You've no doubt read and enjoyed Bill Tidy's Fosdyke Saga, the cartoon strip subsidised by the Tripe Marketing Board. And still you haven't tumbled to the fact that the North is invading, and trying to take over, and trying to impose their bluff, no-nonsense, friendly, gritty, Boycottish values on our effete, arty-farty-Dartington, southern way of life.

I only tumbled last week. I was up in Leeds, doing a job for Yorkshire TV (bet you didn't know they had TV up in

61

Yorkshire, did you? Oh aye, they have, and they're making programmes, by heck, and I don't know why I'm sounding like a bloody northerner except that so many TV programmes these days come from the North that after a while you can't help it – it's another warning sign) and during the lunch-break, sorry, dinner-break, I was taken to the bar for a quick 'un. The bar was lined with those little plastic boxes with tiny levers on that have replaced beer-pulls, labelled Reg Smith's Mighty Brew, Pennine Hair-Grower, Tad Smith's First Prize Leek Show Special, Bill Smith's Right Upper Cut, Theakston's Old Weird 'n' Wonderful, Geoff Smith's Faggotmaster and so on, and on the point of meekly succumbing to this brash, brassy display I suddenly rebelled.

'A pint of cider, please,' I asked.

A moment of consternation. The barmaid (tough, tired blonde with ready wit and cauliflower ears) looked it up in her dictionary and rummaged for a while in the exotic drinks shelf, among the pineapple juice and Southern Comfort. Eventually she found some. Theakston's Odd 'n' Unaccountable Cider. Or very similar.

'Will this do?' she sneered.

"Aye, reet, 'appen it will,' I said coolly.

She poured out two small bottles into a pint glass. Then before my very eyes she added to the cider three lumps of ice, two slices of lemon, a cherry on a stick and a small object which could either have been a glass eye or a pickled onion, though I suppose it were an onion, as there's something a bit effete about a glass eye. I was just about to say that I could take the cider without the salad when a voice behind me said warningly:-

'Better say nothing, lad. Oop here, cider's a nancy's drink.'

That's when I tumbled. To the fact that the North *is* making a take-over bid. Not only are they invading us down here with their beer and comedians and mushy tripe and cricketers and James Herriot in *When The Vet Comes Home*, but they are rejecting *our* culture up there. Cider a nancy's drink, indeed! I defy anyone to call cider a nancy's drink at its present price. Come to that, I defy anyone to say he's heard the word 'nancy' for a few years down south; it's only up in the hairy-chested North you hear old-fashionedness like that.

Now, it's no good us in the South trying to pretend, as we usually do, that we can be as tough, brash, warm and gritty if we try. That's just playing into their hands. What we've got to do is, for once, play up to our soft, camp, effete, la-di-da, highbrow image. As their tanks of beer roll down the motorway, the juggernauts should be coming the other way from the South loaded to the gunwales with all those products associated with the South - cider, Oxford marmalade, Perrier water, China tea, muffins, croissants, cigarette-holders, silk dressing gowns and Instant Sunshine records. The slogans should be written to match. 'Oxford Marmalade. Not bad at all, actually.' ... 'Perrier takes hair off your chest.' ... 'Croissants are a girl's breakfast!' – and why ever not? 'Cider! After all it's a nancy's drink!'

All wrong for the North? I'm not so sure. All this tough, gritty stuff, this feeling that *haute cuisine* can aim no higher than pork scratchings, it's a bit of a cover-up really. It's the way people behave when they've got secret doubts and worries about their masculinity. It almost reminds me of Australia, where men strut about, even worse than in the North of England, with a can of lager in each pocket, and they're all secretly longing to be ballet dancers or opera singers, which is what they all turn into as soon as they leave. It's a great effort being gritty and tough all the time, you know.

Remember John Conteh, Northerner of the Year in 1979? It turns out that he *hated* boxing, dreaded getting in the ring. He now much prefers drinking and crying on girls' shoulders. Remember that MP who was so confused by being a northerner that he had to call a press conference every week just to find out which woman he was living with? They couldn't stand the strain of being tough and northern.

Do you want to know what a northerner is like when he owns up? Like David Hockney, that's who – arty, rich, successful and apparently free from stress. And living 5,000 miles from Bradford.

Here's my idea for a TV commercial. It's a grey, rainy afternoon in a northern street. A man is trudging along the pavement, his rather nice silk Italian jacket with its collar turned up. He opens a door and goes inside. Inside, we see him come in. It's Russell Harty. He flicks a drop of his rain from his eyelashes.

Harty: 'Oooh, what a bitch of a day, isn't it? Once a week I have to come up to Manchester to do my little show, and I just *know* it's going to teem down. Honestly, how people can live up here! Luckily, I know I can get through my day in Manchester because I know I've got my …'

Lapsang Souchong? Hot water bottle? Smoked salmon butty? It doesn't really matter. As long as we start to give the northerners the chance to come out and be the nice softies they're all longing to be. Poor old things.

Meanwhile, because this will take a little while to get off the ground, there's something we can all do. There's one thing that all northerners agree on, and that is that the North starts twenty miles south of where they come from. To a bloke from Leeds, Manchester is a midlands town. To an inhabitant of York, Leeds hardly qualifies for the north, while a Geordie would consider the lot of them pretend southerners. We have to play on this and maintain that the North always starts twenty miles *north* of where they come from. That'll worry them.

Unfortunately, we mostly have no idea where places are up there. So here's a little list to memorise, starting at the bottom and going up. Nottingham, Sheffield, Leeds, Middlesborough, Newcastle, Berwick. To make it easier, remember it as NSLMNB. Or, even easier, as Norman Smith's Light Medium Nauseous Beers.

Women's Humour

Today I propose to deal with the most dangerous topic in the world. Are women humorous? If not, why not? And if so, why do they always muck-up the punch-line?

I know it is a dangerous topic, because for years I have partaken in the following conversation at dinner parties, supper parties and all those other occasions where women are allowed to be aggressive.

She: Why don't magazines print more women humorists?

Me: Well, really, actually, you see, I think it's because women aren't always that, well, funny, really.

She: That is a vile sexist remark. I would offer violence to you, if I were a man.

Me: If you were a man, though, you would agree with me about women humorists.

She: *(Slap.)*

I have in recent years revised the script of this conversation to read somewhat differently. It now goes like this.

She: Why don't magazines print more women humorists?

Me: Humour is basically produced by people who are

insecure, fantasists, escapists, and irresponsible. They are making up for some deep lack. Women on the other hand are too sensible and practical to need humour. It's only men, poor things, who have to take refuge in humour.

She: Hmm. At first sight that seems plausible and even flattering. But deep down it's a vile sexist remark, I'm afraid. (*Slap*.)

And yet humour is so easy. All you have to do is work out your own variation on the banana skin joke. Although nobody has ever seen anyone fall over on a banana skin, this has for some reason been elected as the prime example of a joke. The basic variation on it is somebody walking along towards a banana skin and then, because everyone knows he's going to fall over, *not* falling over. It's after that stage that you have to work out your own version.

The Monty Python banana skin joke, for example, would go

like this. A man walks along a pavement towards a banana skin. He avoids it. Ten paces later a huge banana twelve feet long falls out of the skin and crushes him.

Woody Allen is different. Woody Allen would walk along the pavement and see a banana lying in front of him. He picks it up. The banana then rejects him.

I don't know if you've been to the Comedy Strip where alternative comedy takes place, but they would have their very own version of the banana joke based on the hairy-chested and skinhead view of life, like this. A man walks along a pavement and sees a banana. 'Christ,' he says, 'it's a f … ing banana.' He then slips over on a pile of dog shit.

You can even imagine bananas being worked into Irish jokes.

'Why would an Irishman eat a banana?'

'I don't know. Why would an Irishman eat a banana?'

'He wouldn't. Unless he was given political status first.'

Now, how would a woman approach this situation? We have the picture already. A woman. A pavement. A banana skin, The woman walks along. She *doesn't* fall over, because that would be undignified, and she would be an object of ridicule, especially to men, and that would never do.

So let's think. She walks along. She sees the banana and she picks it up. Then she says something. She says: 'Typical! Always having to clear up after men.'

No, that doesn't work somehow. Yet the secret is there somewhere. After all, the banana joke is as old as the hills. It even turns up in the fragments of Latin comedies. Here is a fragment of an old Latin comedy I happen to have with me.

Marcus: Why, look, here comes Aurelius.

Gratius: And he is walking straight towards that banana skin.

Marcus: With any luck he will slip over on it and fall.

Gratius: That would be funny!

(Enter Aurelius. He falls over on the banana and kills himself.)

Gratius and Marcus: Ho ho ho! Ha ha ha!

Now, what does that tell us? It tells us for a start that the Romans had a fairly cruel sense of humour. Also that they had a fairly primitive sense of humour. But most important of all, since bananas were totally unknown in Roman times, it tells us that what we have here is a forgery, and that someone has gone to the bother of imitating an old Roman comedy. Who would bother to do that? Amazing.

No, the only safe way to become a humorist or comedian is the way it's always been done, and that is to be so small at school that you get bullied, and the only way out of being bullied is to make people laugh. That's how Woody Allen started. That's how Dudley Moore started. Of course, some people are so small and insignificant that nobody even bothers to bully them. The only way that they can get recognition is by *writing* something funny, usually for the teacher. The teacher then stands up in class and says how funny your writing is, and why can't the rest of the class do something original like that? *Then* you *really* get bullied, good and proper. That's how I started as a humorist. I used to bully people, good and proper, all these small people who wrote funny things, even though I suffered from being normal size, which is a handicap I shall never really get over.

Anyway, I've now come to the definitive version of my dinner party script. It goes like this.

She: Why don't magazines print more women humorists?

Me: That's a vile sexist remark! (*Beats her over the head with a banana.*)

Getting Away From It All

The first day you come back from holiday, you switch on the radio to hear the news and someone says: 'The Turkish hi-jack is over at last ...' and you feel really pleased. Not because the Turkish hi-jack is over at last, but because you've no idea that there was a Turkish hi-jack and you couldn't care less. One of the great things about being on holiday is that there is no news. Last year in South America I missed entirely the SAS siege of the Iranian consulate and President Carter's bid to rescue the hostages, and I'm not sorry. For a while, actually, I was under

68

the impression that President Carter had sent in helicopters to rescue the Iranian consulate, which was under siege by the SAS, but all his helicopters crashed in Hyde Park, and I think it made marginally a better story.

And local papers on holiday aren't much help. In all the time I was there the Latin American papers only carried two items with English connections. One was the death of Hitchcock. The other was something about the Queen, and that I almost missed, as to them she is known unaccountably as Queen Isabel.

However, if you really do miss the news while you're away, I've prepared a short list of major items which will happen in your absence. Cut it out and keep it with your sunglasses and Ambre Solaire.

The Turkish hi-jack. Seven armed men take over a jumbo jet at Cairo and demand that it be flown to Rome. They promise to release the hostages in exchange for a) £1m and b) a chance to run the Italian government. They are gladly given the chance to run the Italian government, but after two days of moderate rule they fall on a vote of confidence. They demand to be flown to Istanbul in exchange for a) £1m and b) the release of all political prisoners everywhere. Then one of the hi-jackers makes the mistake of pinching a stewardess's bottom; all the hi-jackers are overpowered by enraged stewardesses and the Turkish hi-jack is over at last.

A day's play is lost in the Test due to rain, and it looks like a draw now.

The man with five hearts dies. In a revolutionary operation to give a heart patient as many hearts as possible, surgeons mistakenly connect the green lead to the live terminal and the patient short-circuits.

The 8.47 from Shenfield to Liverpool Street is cancelled.

Nuclear war is narrowly averted when Julius K Neipsheimer, the new Secretary of State for Military Adventures, denies having said at a dinner party that America should bomb the hell out of the Russians. What he actually said was that the Russian Chef had made a hell of a good bombe.

The Russians march into Poland. In a surprise countermove, the Poles march into Russia. The match is adjourned overnight and both sides agree to settle for a draw. When you return from holidays, all is as before.

Mrs Thatcher goes on Desert Island Discs and subjects Mr Plomley to a long and intense interrogation about his life story.

Benn says it again. Healey slams Benn. Benn is unrepentant. Foot slams Benn. Benn says it again. Harold Wilson says he would have slammed Benn. The media slam Benn. Benn slams the media. Then all is forgotten because of death of man with five hearts.

Boy, was her face red! When Shirley Wilkins, 19, of Croydon, answered her parents' phone she had little idea that the voice at the other end would be that of Prince Charles. No – Prince Charles hadn't rung her up, he merely had a wrong number and he was trying to reach Lady Diana. He was very nice, said Shirley later, and joked about how being in the Royal Family didn't help you with the phone service. We chatted about Croydon a bit, which he'd once visited to open a factory, and asked me about my work as a temp secretary. I told him I was going to watch him getting married on TV, and he joked that the wedding wouldn't have cost the taxpayer anything if only he and Lady Diana got Equity fees for appearing. Then he said he would like to send me a ticket for the big occasion but he thought they'd all be gone. Then he sort of rang off.

The Palace later confirmed that Prince Charles did sometimes dial his own numbers.

The day you come back from holiday, the papers announce a total shutdown at Heathrow because of a customs go-slow. You should know. You're sitting at Heathrow reading the papers.

Keeping One's Eyes Peeled

The other day I was passing along Oxford Street (which is about the best thing you can do to Oxford Street) when a wild wailing sound struck my ear. The odd thing was that it wasn't a police car. It was a set of bagpipes. Somewhere opposite John

Lewis a busker was playing the pipes. I soon spotted him. There was a large empty space on the pavement round him. The only other person occupying it was a motor bicycle messenger dressed in the usual modern jousting equipment – space helmet, inflatable plastic jacket, black gauntlets, frayed jeans and oxy-acetylene welder's goggles – and talking down his microphone to head office. What the man in head office was obviously saying was, 'I don't believe there's a bloody bagpipe player in Oxford Street!', because as I passed, the motor cyclist beckoned the bagpipe player over to blow a few bars into his walkie-talkie set. The man at head office was definitely convinced, judging from the reaction.

It all looked quite natural at the time, but if someone had said to me: 'What are the chances of seeing a man playing a bagpipe into a motorbike in Oxford Street during the rush hour?', I would have given him very favourable odds against. 1,000-1, maybe. Or, in an I-Spy test, about a total of 560 points.

Here, to enliven your journeys through London, are other sights you might just see if you keep your eyes open, with points allotted for each.

A trailing house plant growing in the back window of a parked car (400).

A policeman walking along (1), *in shirt-sleeves* (10), *with a walkie-talkie pinned to his shoulder* (1), *listening to Radio 1* (400).

A man giving up his seat in the Tube to a woman (600).

A girl giving up her seat in the Tube to a woman (400).

An evening paper placard reading: 'OBSCURE ACTRESS DIES' (5,000).

A traffic warden (1), *writing out a ticket* (1), *being begged by the driver not to book him* (1) *and tearing up the ticket* (3,000).

Anyone holding open the door to a big department store and being thanked for it (800).

A person playing an instrument in the street with no visible means of collecting money for it (5,000).

A flower tub with no litter in (4,000).

A litter bin with no flowers in (0).

A person on roller skates (10).

A person on roller skates with ear-phone music (20).

Two people on roller skates with ear-phone music going down opposite sides of the street throwing a frisbee to each other (100).

71

A plainclothes policeperson on roller skates with ear-phone music arresting two roller-skaters with ear-phone music throwing a frisbee across the street to each other (4,000).

Unless it's being done for a film (400).

A jean shop with no music in it (400,000).

A person in a non-smoking section of Tube or bus asking a smoker to put out their cigarette (100).

And succeeding (1,000).

A person in a smoking compartment angrily asking a non-smoker if he would kindly refrain from non-smoking (10,000).

The person you live with or are married to, walking down Oxford Street when you know they're meant to be in Sidcup for the day (500), arm in arm with another friend of yours (—500).

A person with a British passport actually putting litter into a litter bin (700).

A person with litter actually putting a British passport into a litter bin (7,000).

A tramp going through a litter bin (10) and finding a pair of sun-glasses, British passport, ticket to Miami and packet of cigars (1,000) and just taking the cigars (10).

A policeman sleeping rough in a doorway (5,000) who turns out not to be a policeman at all (10) but a plainclothes tramp (5,000).

A shop with a notice saying FINAL WEEKS - EVERY-THING MUST GO! which you know to your certain knowledge has been there for a month (10), a year (10), or five years (11).

A man in a shop window taking down a sign saying STILL ONLY £10.99! and putting up one saying STILL ONLY £15.99! (99).

A bicyclist being breathalysed (400).

Two people of the same sex walking hand in hand (800).

A policeman and policewoman walking hand in hand (8,000).

A very famous person (4,000).

A very famous person walking hand in hand with a police-woman (10,000).

Or, indeed, anyone looking remotely happy (from 500 to 50,000 depending on the state of bliss).

Anglo-Scottish Understanding

Q   *What is a Scot?*
A   A person who comes from north of the border.
Q   *Why does he come from north of the border?*
A   He cannot stand living north of the border, so he comes south.
Q   *Where to?*
A   King's Cross.
Q   *And then?*
A   The nearest bar to King's Cross.
Q   *Do the Scots drink a lot?*
A   Yes, they drink a lot.
Q   *Why?*
A   Because they cannot stand living north of the border.
Q   *But surely Scots are very patriotic?*
A   As soon as they get to King's Cross, yes. They love Scotland when they are somewhere else.
Q   *What do they think of the English?*
A   They hate them. They blame everything that goes wrong on the English. They would love to be shot of the English, except for one thing.
Q   *What's that?*
A   Then they couldn't blame the English any more. The Scots would hate to run their own country.
Q   *Why?*
A   Because it's only being run from London that keeps them united. Independent, they'd be at each other's throats in a moment.
Q   *How do you know?*
A   Because they always were till the English took the place over.
Q   *Who is the most famous Scot of all time?*
A   Prince Albert. He invented the kilt, tartans, Scottish country dancing, Highland games and Hogmanay.

Q *Is that true?*

A Nearly.

Q *You don't like the Scots, do you?*

A ' On the contrary. They are warm-hearted, lively, poetic, mercurial, creative, good companions and fiercely loyal.

Q *Anything else?*

A Yes – drunk.

Q *What do Scots like most?*

A Defeat. The most glorious dates in Scottish history are almost all times when the English did them down – the '15, the '45, the death of Mary Queen of Scots, the Glencoe Massacre.

Q *Do they want revenge?*

A No – just a good grouse and a chance to get drunk.

Q *What is the happiest period of a Scotsman's life?*

A The period between qualifying gloriously for the World Cup finals and their disastrous exit from the World Cup finals.

Q *Why is Robbie Burns so popular in Scotland?*

A Because the English cannot understand him.

Q *Why do the Scots wear the kilt?*

A They don't. Only Perthshire landowners wear the kilt, and they are all English – at least, they all have English accents and live in England. They only go back to Scotland for the mating season.

Q *When is that?*

A When they are drunk.

Q *What are the good things about Scotland?*

A Whisky, kippers, fresh rolls, mountains, a good haggis.

Q *What are the bad things about Scotland?*

A Drinking whisky with lemonade, finding bones in kippers, getting fat on fresh rolls, getting lost on mountains, a bad haggis. And the bagpipes.

Q *Why are all Scots called Mac?*

A They are not. They are all called Jummie. New York taxi passengers are all called Mac.

Q *What are Scots good at?*

A Showbiz, farming, fishing, football, arguing, defeat and getting drunk.

Q *How does a Scotsman get famous?*

A A Scotsman never gets famous. If he makes it big in Scotland they all say, Well, he will never make it big in London.

Q   *And if he does?*
A   They say he's sold out and disown him.
Q   *Is that why Billy Connolly gets drunk?*
A   No comment.
Q   *What is the difference between Glasgow and Edinburgh?*
A   A short motorway and a total lack of comprehension.
The people of Edinburgh are popularly supposed to be a lot of
cold fish, a twee middle-crowd living in one of the most
beautiful cities in Europe. Glaswegians are said to be a warm,
vital crowd living in a bombsite. The ideal city, so it is said,
would be Edinburgh inhabited by Glaswegians.
Q   *Would it work?*
A   Only until the first Saturday night.
Q   *What is the Auld Alliance?*
A   The ancient bond between France and Scotland.
Q   *Based on what?*
A   The fact that the French don't like the English either.
Q   *Why, if Scotland is about the same size as England, are
there so many fewer people in Scotland?*
A   Partly because so many Scots have come from north of
the border. Partly because most of Scotland is uninhabitable,
outside Glasgow, Edinburgh, a few other towns and some
farming areas.
Q   *So you wouldn't recommend me going there?*
A   Far from it! Scotland is a tremendous place. The people
are great, the country is great, the architecture is great and the
licensing laws are twice as good as ours.
Q   *So why have you been saying all these terrible things
about ...?*
A   To please the Scots, of course, you twit. There's nothing
they like better than being misunderstood by the English. It's
the only thing that makes them feel superior.
Q   *The only thing?*
A   Apart from getting smashed out of their minds, of
course.

The Age-Old Four-Letter Word

Your head is all muzzy. There's a thin film of red over your eyes. You keep growling to yourself and shaking your head in fury. Sometimes you feel like running out into the street, kicking all the dustbins over and spraying passers by with hand grenades. You tighten your hands till the nails hurt.

You know what the trouble is, don't you?

You're in love again.

Ah, love! Why does it always come with the wrong symptoms? Why don't bells ring and lights shine? More specifically, why doesn't *he* ring? Why doesn't he notice when you make a special effort? Why does he never measure up to you? Why doesn't he just go and take a running jump?

A famous Frenchman once said: 'True love is like a ghostly apparition. Everyone tells ghost stories, but very few people have actually seen a ghost.' Doctors now think that the famous Frenchman was confusing two different kinds of love. One is true love, which is rare. The other is ordinary love, which is a disease, mostly composed of withdrawal symptoms. It strikes first in early childhood, when you love your parents. Growing up is a process of withdrawing from them.

'I love my parents, of course, but I do find them incredibly annoying and impossible to get through to, and they simply don't understand me.' What is wrong with that statement? The word 'but' is wrong. The statement should read: 'I love my parents, of course, *therefore* I find them incredibly annoying,' etc. Love is the wonderful feeling that you have met someone who can fulfil all your requirements, followed by the long, slow process of discovering he can't.

It never occurs to you that you're not measuring up to his requirements. That's because, as doctors have now found out, love affects the eyes, causing short-sightedness, rosy vision, blindness to the obvious and tears. Tears of sorrow, sometimes. Tears of rage, more often. But mostly tears of frustration that things aren't going the way you want, that he isn't turning out to be the person you want, or even worse, that he is turning out for some other person.

Tears of self-pity, in fact.

Your head is all clear. You jump out of the bed in the morning, raring to go. You think of all the things you would like to do and you get round to doing at least some of them. You feel an inner surge of energy, and things look twice as good as usual.

You know what the trouble is, don't you?

You're not in love.

Doctors now know that this is the danger period, the time when love may most easily strike you down, the stage when you think what a smashing person you are, that it might be fun to share it all with someone else. And before you know where you are the microbes have crept into your system, and some perfectly ordinary bloke has infected you, and rosy vision sets in, and you are suffering from love again.

You will try to find a scientific explanation, of course. Your star signs are matching. You are very like each other. You are very different from each other. You have the same interests. You have complementary, that is to say completely different, interests. There is some chemistry at work. Or maybe algebra. Perhaps even geography.

Unfortunately, doctors have now discovered that love affects the ears. It makes you hear only the things you want to hear, and ignore everything else. It makes you deaf to common sense, experience and warning signs. Above all, it makes you deaf to friends saying: 'I don't know what she sees in him' or 'Doesn't she realise what she's letting herself in for?' It's no use friends saying this to your face, because it's the kind of thing that parents say, and you love your parents so you don't listen to them.

You know all this is true. I know all this is true. But it won't stop you, or me, sickening for love and becoming blind and deaf.

Doctors have no idea why it still happens.

After all, it happens to doctors all the time.

Normal Business Practices

Ah, Deborah. Come in. Yes, sit down. Well, I hope? That cold cleared up? Good, good. Don't want winter colds going round the office already.

Now, I'll come straight to the point. I am afraid I have to give you your notice. I am doing this very reluctantly and unwillingly, as I hate to lose anyone from the organisation especially at a time of unemployment, but I think you will agree that you simply aren't fitting in here. It's not just a question of personality, though that comes into it; it's the fact that you don't seem to be able to cope with the work and don't even seem to want to cope.

Certainly I will give you an example. I wanted to give you some letters to do on Friday at 4.30, but you had already left. Your contract specifies that you should be here till 5.30. Nor is this the first time …

That is not the point. I had had a long business lunch and the traffic was very thick, so I could not return before 4.30. As an executive I am sometimes forced to have long boring meetings over lunch, and afterwards I have to work as hard as possible to catch up.

Yes, sometimes I go straight on from Friday lunch to home. As you very well know, it takes ages to get to my place in Wiltshire and my wife and I like to leave well before the rush hour.

But this is not the point. As a secretary, your job is to be here during your working hours, ready to do work when called upon. Sometimes you complain of too little work, and sometimes too much. Surely doing a few letters at 4.30 cannot be called driving you round the bend with overwork?

No, I certainly do not remember any occasion on which I have come back stinking of garlic, giving off brandy fumes and attempting to force my loathsome advances on you. The whole thing is quite ludicrous. Why on earth should I want to? What scrap of evidence could you possibly have that such an unlikely event took place?

I did not know you had a tape recorder. The firm has not given you a tape recorder. You have your own tape recorder. I see. No, I would not be interested in hearing any of your tape recordings. It is quite beside the point. I am merely pointing out to you that I am very dissatisfied with your work and am disposing of your services.

Certainly I can give you another example. On Friday, at 4.30, in your absence when I was still here hard at work, I had occasion to look out a very important letter to a chairman of another company, as it was of somewhat confidential nature. I do not think much of your filing system, Deborah; that letter was nowhere to be seen. All you have to do is type and keep letters. You do not seem capable of doing either.

Why on earth would you want to keep that letter in your own home? It is of no conceivable interest to anyone but me. It is merely expressing interest in the activities of another company.

Yes, I suppose that I can imagine that our chairman might be upset to learn that I was looking for a better paid post elsewhere, but how could he possibly find out? By seeing the letter. Which you might have to send to him. I see.

This clumsy attempt at blackmail rather depresses me, Deborah. I haven't got where I am in business without having to deal with the odd spot of skullduggery and dirty practice, you know. You simply don't know me if you think I am going to succumb to blackmail.

Then what would you call it?

You would call it normal business practice.

I do not call it normal practice. I am not in the habit of going around blackmailing people into doing what I want them to do.

The Chambers deal. Yes, there may have been a small element of blackmail in the Chambers deal. Yes, there may have been a large element of blackmail in the Chambers deal. But that surely is going back before your time? How on earth could you know about the Chambers deal?

From Miss Whetstone.

With whom I had a close friendship.

Very close? It may have been. I cannot remember.

It may interest you to know, Deborah, that whatever may or may not have passed been Miss Whetstone and me is now at an end, and is a closed chapter.

Not to Miss Whetstone.

I see.

Yes, I vaguely remember writing letters to her. You will be disappointed to hear, Deborah, that she returned them all to me and I destroyed them.

But not before taking copies.

I did not know that.

Well, Deborah, I am a busy man and do not have time to go on with this petty argument, so let me just say that I am going to give you one last chance but that if your work does not improve I shall be forced to rethink my position. For the time being, you can get on with the letters left over from Friday, which I was forced to write out in long hand in your absence.

At a higher salary.

Yes, I think I could offer you another £200 a year.

Another £1,000. Yes, I think we could manage that.

Now I must go off to lunch. It may turn out to be a long one. No, don't bother. I'll do anything that has to be done when I get back.

Yes, I too am glad we've had this little talk.

The Dangerous World of Relationships

Having survived innumerable liaisons, many a tragic affair, several lifelong romances, five marriages and a very long evening with a female Romanian architect, I think I may be said to have an average experience of relationships. And the golden truth I have learnt about relationships, whether they are with the opposite sex, the same sex, a pet or even a house plant, is that they do not come to grief on the big things like love, money, ambition and sex so often as on the small things like personal habits, attitudes, prejudices and sex.

This is because people rush blindly into relationships without doing adequate research. Oh yes, they establish that they're in love; that they enjoy each other's company; that they have the same attitude to life, television and Woody Allen; that they think this is a wonderful relationship which is going to last for ever and ever. Well, that's the basic requirement, the very least you need. What they *haven't* found out is what the other person thinks about party games, puddings, bending paperbacks back as you read them and throwing old newspapers away. The really crucial things, in fact.

Many a wonderful relationship has been ruined because two otherwise well-suited people were totally incompatible in the little matter of, say, temperature. I know one couple whose marriage, has, against all the odds, survived the fact that he

likes a sheet and a blanket at night and she likes four blankets, a duvet and socks. It has survived long enough for their children to be now starting university. At last they can break loose and do some travelling. The only trouble is – and it looks likely to wreck the marriage – he can only go north and she has to go to the tropics.

So if you are thinking of combining with someone in the near future and expect them to say those magic words: 'Would you care to initiate a relationship with me?' for heaven's sake make sure you are compatible first. Make them fill in a questionnaire; hold an informal audition; talk to their parents; *but find out first.*

To help you, I have mapped out the areas in which most relationships are later found floating upside down, without a crew and with all the lifeboats gone.

1. Listening to music. Most people don't listen to music completely without reaction, except music critics. They tap feet, click fingers or nod in time with the music. Or, of course, very nearly but not quite in time with the music. Some people hum along, just audibly. A few people sit motionless for up to fifteen minutes, then say loudly: 'Ye-eah!' I myself have an appalling habit of clicking my teeth in complicated rhythms. It's quite inaudible when there's music playing, but when I'm remembering a favourite record, all people can hear is tuneless grinding of molars, unaware that I'm really bashing out the most exotic rhythmic patterns. I'm thinking of making the big switch to electric dentures.

Anyway, remember that where you now watch your loved one enthralled by a record and think how wonderful it is to see someone so enraptured, you will one day say to yourself: 'If he doesn't stop swaying backwards and forwards with his eyes shut, I shall scream till the neighbours come.' Ask him to stop *now.*

2 The world is divided into people who like party games, and those who would rather die than get involved. One from the first camp should not live with one from the second camp. The same is roughly true of community singing, wearing fancy dress and putting your hand up when volunteers from the audience are asked for.

3. Money. The world is also divided into people who feel sick if they get into debt, and people who don't know what it's like to be without an overdraft. If you are one of each, you could still make it, but for God's sake have separate bank accounts.

4. Nightwear. Some people always put it on, some never. I don't think it's anything to do with sensuality; it's another facet of the hot v cold problem. But you've both got to decide to do the same thing. If one person sleeps with nothing on, the other person is going to feel perpetually overdressed, which is something we shouldn't have to worry about after we've got undressed. A friend of mine once had a brief liaison with a girl

83

with very poor circulation who wore a dressing gown in bed. 'Nothing wrong with that,' he said, 'except that every time she turned over things fell out of her pockets. I hurt myself badly on a hairbrush one night.' I personally think girls in pyjamas are rather attractive, but that's my problem.

5. Throwing things away. Some do, some don't. If the two types live together, you sooner or later find one partner routinely going through the waste paper baskets and dustbins to find what the other is trying to get rid of. If you feel now a flash of irritation when your partner says: 'You never know when it might come in useful,' your relationship is already doomed.

6. Arguments. An argument should ideally take place in order to get at the truth, but unfortunately a lot of people (mostly men, I'm afraid) argue to win, and will go on backing a half-baked idea until the other person bursts into tears or throws something. Unfortunately, in the early stages of relationships, when the sun is shining, there aren't any arguments and it's hard to know how things will turn out. Better provoke an argument early on, just to see how it goes.

7. Does he like the countryside? Do you hate it? Or vice versa? Then call it off now.

8. Some people skip starters in order to leave room for the pudding. Others order every course except the pudding. Put one of each kind together, and most of your meals will be spent with one partner staring into space. Unless, of course, you compromise by both having every course, in which case laying the foundations for a very overweight middle-aged couple.

9. Sex. Not as important as eating, but still quite important. A New Yorker once told me: 'A good sex life takes up less than five percent of your time; a rotten sex life takes up all your time.' I can't better that. She then added reflectively: 'My mother told me that.'

10. Funny stories. Why is it that so many partnerships sort themselves out sooner or later into a double act, consisting of one person telling stories badly and the other correcting them the whole time? Because they didn't get it sorted out right at the beginning. It's one of the facts of life that we find ourselves telling stories more often than we have a stock of stories for; therefore we start telling the same anecdotes over and over again. The other person must understand this, and at

least hope that the anecdotes improve with age. *Don't interrupt.*
Realise humbly that you don't do it any better either.

There is one exception to all this; the person who believes
that stories are funnier if you say everything three times, like
this: 'It was a lovely day, blue sky, not a cloud to be seen. And
this man, just an ordinary bloke, some fellow or other, was
strolling along, just walking down the street, minding his own
business when suddenly, out of the blue, from nowhere ...' Or,
if it's personal reminiscence: 'I remember one time we were
staying in this hotel in Brussels, ordinary Belgian hotel, usual
continental pension ...'

People like that should not have a relationship with anyone.

The Value of Cutting Comments

I recently made the light-hearted though perceptive point that
relationships are more likely to be terminated by the little
irritations in life, not the big things.

I did not know how true it was, until the young person with
whom I had been sharing my life screamed: 'This is the last
straw! You are just using our relationship as raw material for
articles in magazines!'

'My dear,' I said suavely. 'The article was about the little
irritations of life. I did not mention you at all. By any standards
you are one of the major irritations of life.'

She must have taken this as a personal criticism, for not a
minute later she was sweeping out of my life for ever, taking
with her all her possessions and my jewellery. She paused only
to say: 'Now at last you can sit up all night cutting bits out of
newspapers without driving me round the bend!'

It's true. I do tend to cut things out of newspapers.
Interviews. Reviews of books I ought to buy. Unusually good
cartoons. Recipes. Then, when I want them later, I know
exactly where they are. They're in that huge pile of unsorted
newspaper cuttings over there.

On the night she left I sat up late, as usual, going through newspapers, and found a copy of the *Guardian*. On page 8 of this paper I found a piece by Rachel Billington which was headed 'Englishmen are afraid of fiction'. That sounded interesting. I cut the piece out and read it.

Well, what she says certainly is interesting. She says that women love fiction because they need it – it is an extension of their emotional life. Men avoid fiction because they prefer facts, reality, useful information. She quotes a survey which shows that this starts very early on in life; apparently young girls go for fiction but boys only for comics. 'Comics are all surface. No emotion demanded there.'

She refers fleetingly to men's escapist reading, which she says is either military history or pornography, but says that the latter subject is far too complicated to discuss here and returns immediately to women and fiction. 'Mills and Boon or Anna Karenina, it's the same root, same effect,' she says. Emotion. People. Relationships. Cutting bits out of newspapers, when I could be having a relationship. Where did my life go wrong? A silent tear rolled down my cheek and fell on a week-old copy of the *Standard*, about to be cut up by the butcher's knife.

But hold on! I cried. Mrs Billington has missed a point there. You cannot dismiss pornography so easily. Pornography is a male-oriented fantasy wish-fulfilment thing of which the chief criticism is that it reduces women to the level of objects. But surely the same is true of much women's fiction; using emotion instead of sex, it reduces men to the level of cardboard cut-outs on which the flickering light of female fantasy plays. A girl I once wanted to marry told me that she had just read a novel which contained the – to her – perfect man. Of course I read it immediately. It was by Monica Dickens, a good writer, his name was Sam and he was kind, supportive, reliable, glamorous, perfect and always there when you needed him. He was also totally faceless, with no character or interest whatsoever. (I felt far superior. I married her immediately.)

I also resent the implication that men are uninterested in, or incapable of, emotional fantasy. Given a moment's thought, I'm sure I could come up with something …

'Miles, I don't know if you've met Rachel Billington?'

I turned as my host spoke, and found myself looking into a pair of intensely deep eyes. I knew, somehow, that this was the novelist I had always wanted to meet. Suddenly, words seemed hard to find.

'Lost your tongue, Miles?' laughed my host. 'My goodness, I think your novels have had quite an effect on him. Well, I'll leave you two to talk about it.'

'I … I haven't really read your novels,' I stammered. 'I tend only to read histories of the Peninsular War, lives of Wellington, stuff like that.'

'And pornography?' she twinkled.

'I think that's a bit complicated to discuss here, don't you?'

'Just what I always say,' she said, looking at me with a new respect. 'But you must try reading novels. They're about people and emotion and life.'

'I'm scared to,' I admitted. 'I'd probably end up cutting bits out of them and putting them in a huge pile.'

'Well, at least that's better than cutting bits out of newspapers. Such a typically male attitude – more and more useless facts. Men are such superficial creatures!'

'On the other hand,' I objected, 'if I didn't cut bits out of papers, I wouldn't have read your *Guardian* piece and we wouldn't be here together in this fantasy.'

'Thank you for nothing,' she said icily. 'We've only just met and already you're using me as material for an article. No wonder that girl ran out on you last week.'

'Look that was only another fantasy,' I said. But she wasn't listening. Another couple had joined us.

'Do you know Harold Pinter and my sister, Lady Antonia?' she said.

Oh God, I've just remembered. A book was published last month by Hodder and Stoughton called the Anti-Book List, in which fifty writers were asked to tear to bits their least favourite book. As one of the grumpy fifty, I chose to attack a children's book by Antonia Fraser. I still stick to my opinion that it's about the worst-written book outside anything by Gyles Brandreth. But I now have this recurring fantasy that one day I will meet Lady Antonia who will burst into tears on hearing my name and cause Harold Pinter to step forward in shining armour and beat me up. And I don't really want the emotions of that fantasy (fear and cowardice) to clash with the emotions of the fantasy in which her sister Rachel Billington teaches me to enjoy reading novels.

It's an exhausting life, day-dreaming.

The Proper Way To Make Television

Did any of you see that BBC programme the other night about an Indian village? No, I didn't either. But everyone who saw it, or reviewed it, raved about it. And do you know why? Because it didn't have any commentary, or background music, or voice over, or Dimbleby-Attenborough striding through the village, or anything. It just showed you pictures of the village and the people, and let you hear the natural noises. People were stunned. It was a breakthrough, they said.

TV is all about pictures. Unfortunately it's also all about a dread of people switching off. It's about cramming every hole with something going on. It's about filling people's ears the whole time. It's about keeping busy. In other words it's about a total lack of confidence in what you're showing somewhere along the line.

You can see this whenever they televise concerts, the way the camera jumps in and out, looking up the soloist's nostrils, paying a surprise visit to the woodwind, looking down the double basses' collars, zooming in on the conductor's sweaty gesticulations; in other words, distracting attention from the music as much as possible. There's nothing very visual about an orchestra and looking at it in close-up makes it less, not more, attractive. When I'm at a concert, which isn't that often, I look anywhere but at the musicians. That's probably why I don't go to concerts. It's such a contrast between the soaring music and the chartered accountants playing it. Maybe that's why gramophone records were such a great invention – it cut out the musicians' faces at last.

If I were in charge of filming a concert, I would give the audience something really worth watching. Like the conductor striding angrily down to the violins and cursing them for getting it wrong. Like the French horn player taking quick swigs from a bottle between solos. Like the double basses reading a book during their hundred bar rest. Like the percussionist picking his nose. Musicians as human beings, in fact.

Either that, or ignoring the orchestra entirely and just having film of a boat going down a river. Ridiculous? Not entirely. It happens sometimes on 'Top of The Pops', when videos depict something almost totally removed from the record which is being played.

The ultimate form of busy television is something like 'Starsky and Hutch', where not a moment passes without tyres squealing, dramatic music nudging your elbow, feet running, guns firing or engines racing. Well, that's all right – if you're going to go over the top, go over the top. It's the programmes that are always clambering to the top without going over that are so irritating. Like the news, which always sounds so urgent and so seldom looks urgent. If I were in charge of news, it would go like this …

Newsreader: (spotlit in an otherwise dramatically black studio) In a bank raid in London today, robbers got away with half a million pounds. (Sound of burning tyres, confused shouting noises. Newsreader licks lips, looks round nervously.) In the get-away, one man who tried to have a go was shot. (A form tip-toes behind the newsreader. Slow, tense music comes up.) Police would like anyone who saw the …

Intruder: Which is the way out?

Newsreader: (getting up) That door over there. But what the …?

Intruder: (puts gun to newsreader's neck) Just go on doing whatever you're doing, nice and slowly. Don't forget I've got you covered. (Walks out of shot.)

Newsreader: Police would like anyone who saw the incident to phone this number … (A shot rings out. Newsreader clutches his shoulder.)

Voice off: I wouldn't give any number if I were you. (Door slams).

Same with political discussions. They should either be entirely natural and full of beautiful pictures, like this …

Chairman: In the studio today I have the Minister of Prosperity and the Shadow spokesman on Prosperity. Minister, what kind of solution do you see to the country's present problems?

Minister: I don't know really. I mean, it's very difficult. I don't really see a way out at the moment.

Chairman: I see. And what about the Opposition?

Spokesman: Well, I must stress that the Government has made a complete hash of things. On the other hand, I've got to admit that we wouldn't do any better.

Chairman: So you have no solutions?

Spokesman: No. Do you?

Chairman: Not that I can think of. So there we have it. As we have twenty-five minutes left, let's have a look at film of life in an Indian village …

Or they should be tremendously busy and over the top, like this.

Chairman: In the studio today, I have the Minister for Prosperity and his Opposition counterpart. Gentlemen, I propose that we avoid the usual exchange of platitude …

Minister: Quite so.

Spokesman: Suits me.

Chairman: ... and let you fight it out to decide a winner.

Minister: You mean – actually *fight?*

Spokesman: Physically? Fight?

Chairman: Certainly. It's the only way we'll ever get a decision.

Minister: I've never heard anything so ...

Spokesman: This is absolutely ...

Chairman: (pulling out a gun) Fight? Or you'll get this.

Minister: Look here, I ... (Chairman fires two shots into the floor. They both leap up. The Labour spokesman lunges forward at the Minister.)

Chairman: And in this middleweight contest to decide if the government is on the right track, the Minister is already locked in an arm-hold. No, he's out of it! And he tries a fore-arm smash! The shadow spokesman, remember, is wearing the suit with the broad stripes ...

TV can occasionally be pure picture. It happens at Wimbledon when, thank God, the commentators shut up during rallies and we can just watch. It happens even more so during snooker games – snooker is the nearest thing to pure television ever invented; the camera seldom moves; there is no music; there is hardly any sound, save for the odd click; and it's wonderful. Morecambe and Wise are at their best just standing in front of a boring curtain, doing their own thing. 'Mastermind' works because the camera has the courage to stay fixed on one person in a chair for a long time.

It might work even better if someone burst in at the end and machine gunned the unsuccessful contestants.

I'll think about that when I'm in charge.

Getting Into The Festive Spirit

Oh God, it's Christmas again. Nothing personal, God, but couldn't you have arranged it some other time of the year, like summer? Yes, I know the Australians get it in summer, and everyone gives each other bikinis and shark-repellent spray, and they have roast turkey on the beach, but what's a few million bronzed Aussies with sand in their Christmas pud compared to the huddled, cold, miserable billions of Northern Europe, all of whom seem to congregate in Oxford Street? I think You should have thought of this first.

(Odd how we always give God a capital letter, as if He would really be impressed by that sort of thing. It must come from some obscure Victorian book of etiquette. 'When addressing correspondence to God, give capital letters to pronouns connected with Him and His close relations. Letters should commence Dear God. If one is conveying a personal rather than business message, it can commence, My Lord, or even – if one is on familiar terms – Lord. It is normal to sign off as Thy Servant. Agnostics may, if they wish, start their correspondence To Whom it may concern, but it is still polite to put a capital W on Whom.')

Thing is, God, that what with You being so busy trying to ward off World War III and get England into the World Cup Finals (well done, by the way, and if You could have done the same for Wales I'd have been ever so grateful), You probably haven't noticed that Christmas is getting slightly out of hand down here. Not exactly the simple little ceremony You planned, with just a few close oxen and asses coming round on the day itself, and the shepherds doing a bit of carol-singing when they could get hold of a sheep-sitter. It's sort of, well, expanded since then.

I think the three wise men was the big mistake, personally. You probably thought at the time, well, nice to give the baby a little start in life with a few gifts: myrrh and frankincense to enjoy now, and some gold to put in the Roman Post Office savings account for later on. Not realising that it was going to escalate into a multi-million pound industry starting in early November with the last posting date for gifts to people on Australian beaches.

Or maybe You genuinely thought that civilisation was going to take root in Australia first? And You really did plan a hot Christmas for us all, with beach cricket and a swim after lunch? Only Homo Sapiens took sudden leave of his senses, and insisted on going to live in the rainswept, damp, slushy north of Europe which You had originally planned as a sort of wild-life park for wolves and bears?

Either way, it would have been nice to have had some warning from the Bible …

16. Mary and Joseph came unto Bethlehem, where the child was to be born.

17. And Mary said unto Joseph, We must send cards to everyone in Nazareth for fear of offending our relations with whom we are not spending the festive season.

18. Joseph replied, saying: And we shall send them gifts, each according to his deserts, down to the least pocket handkerchief and sachet of myrrh.

19. I shall also deck the stable with holly and ivy, assuming there is any left in the market, and get in some wine should any visitors call unexpectedly and order a turkey, and make a pudding, and all those sundry tasks as it is written.

20. Mary approved of all these things, saying to Joseph: It would be nice to have a crib too, you are a carpenter, it should not be too much bother.

21. And Joseph approved of this, saying: If I have the time, if I have the time.

As I said, these are busy times even for Someone as omnipotent and all-seeing as Yourself, so when You next get a chance to rethink Christmas You may welcome a little help over the priorities. With this in mind, I have humbly prepared a short list of the things You may feel like dealing with first.

1. Strings of silver tinsel draped over Japanese electronic goods in shop windows.

2. People singing carols through entryphones.

3. Special Christmas TV shows, especially those with famous people dressed up as Father Christmas.

4. The adoption of the stage coach, robin and turkey as sacred religious symbols.

5. Tape recordings of carols in mainline stations.

6. Snow effects sprayed on to shop windows.

7. Christmas crackers containing functionless plastic objects and the same motto as your neighbour's cracker.

8. So-called humorous books rushed out in September as stocking-fillers.

9. The tune called 'Jingle Bells'.

10. The fact that you cannot send a simple gift without having to pay through the nose for (a) fancy wrapping paper (b) fancy string (c) fancy label (d) fancy sticker saying Happy Xmas (e) fancy stamp costing up to 75p.

11. The habit of estate agents of putting a Christmas stable scene in their window, when you know the real message is: 'Superior mews apartment, needs modernisation, built-in manger, only £50,000.'

12. Plastic mistletoe.

13. Christmas quizzes in newspapers containing unanswerable questions.

I think that once we have cleared up those few problems, we should be well on the way to getting back to what Christmas is all about.

Unless of course I have got the whole thing wrong and You have designed it as a test of character through which we have to pass to emerge better but poorer, colder but wiser. If so, I take it all back.

Though I can't help pointing out that in that case You've let the Australians off pretty lightly.

Thy humble servant, etc, etc.

Messages In The Air

At long last I have shared a car with someone who has a Citizens Band radio, and I can honestly say that listening to him use it has totally changed my life. I now know for sure that I don't want a CB radio. I am very happy for CB freaks to carry on their strange lonely conversations about breakers, good buddies, windows and copying, but I simply don't have the time to learn a new language. It's hard enough keeping the rust off the French I've got.

Anyway, when a CB operator says 'Copy', it only seems to mean, 'I read you', or 'Roger'. So why on earth can't they say Roger? There's a perfectly good lingo left lying about unused since World War II, full of Able Bakers, Angels 15, scramble and direct hit. I admit that it seems somewhat geared to people in aeroplanes shooting each other down, but surely that's a more healthy hobby than sitting in cars in rush hours?

Even more important, we already have a fully operational private language. It's called Using The Telephone. This is a small black object (like a CB radio) which enables you to talk over great distances (like a radio) to people you had no idea even existed (this is called a crossed line, but CB radio seems to be nothing but crossed lines). And the specialised jargon means something quite different from what it says. And there are elaborate formulas, rather like Japanese tea ceremonies, to be gone through before you start speaking.

You'd think a phone conversation should logically start like this.

Me: Miles Kington here.

Caller: Hello, Mr Kington, I have a call for you from the chairman of Hot Drink Machines in answer to your complaint about our tea leaves forecasting an early death for you ...

But this is how it does start, if both of you know the correct rigmarole.

Me: Miles Kington here.

Caller: Hello?

Me: Hello.

Caller: Could I speak to Mr Kington, please?

Me: You are.

Caller: Pardon?

Me: You are.

Caller: I am what?

Me: Speaking to him.

Caller: Oh I'll wait till he comes, then.

But the really important part of Using The Telephone is mastering the all important phrases used. Here is a selection of the most common, with translations in brackets afterwards.

'How are you?' (*I have no interest in your health at all.*)

'Oh, really?' (*And I certainly didn't intend to hear about your jogger's elbow.*)

'Good Lord, well I never.' (*And even if jogger's elbow is caused by bumping into parking meters, I can't see why you think I should be interested, you dreary little hypochondriac.*)

'Funny you should say that, because ...' (*But now we've brought up the subject of health, you're in for three minutes on my sciatic twinge.*)

'Look, I'll tell you why I rang.' (*I am desperately trying to remember why I rang.*)

'Hang on, I'll get a pencil/my diary/a piece of paper.' (*I'm going to the loo.*)

'I'll get back to you on that one.' (*I won't get back to you on that one.*)

'I have a call from Mr Jenkins for you.' (*I have to go and see where Mr Jenkins is, drag him to the phone and hope you haven't rung off, though I wouldn't blame you if you had.*).

'Mr Jenkins is in a meeting.' (*Mr Jenkins is standing right by me, waving his arms and mouthing, 'I can't face him right now'.*)

'Mr Jenkins is on the other line.' (*Mr Jenkins has taken the day off at Sandown.*)

'Hell-o! What a surprise!' (*Oh Christ, it's mother.*)

'I hope I haven't called at an awkward moment.' (*We had lunch early today, so I thought I'd ring in the middle of yours.*)

'No.' (*Yes*).

'Am I interrupting something?' (*I can hear someone talking in the background and I am desperate to know who it is.*)

'No, no.' (*Why do you always ring up in the middle of* '*Brideshead Revisited*'?)

'Charles is fine, thanks.' (*Charles is a swine and we haven't talked for three weeks.*)

'This is a very bad line. Can you ring me back?' (*I think you should pay for part of this call.*)

'Quiero hablar con Señor Montez, por favor.' (*I am not just a wrong number, I am a Spanish wrong number. Nor do I speak any English. This is going to take a long time.*)

'I am not at home at present, but you can leave a message.' (*I have been replaced by a machine.*)

What We Did On Our Holidays

The Print Shop Man

'I run a photocopy shop in Bayswater. Kwikfast, or Fotospeed, something like that. Rather like a large passport photo booth. Yes, they're all the rage. Just install three old photocopy machines and you're away. People will pay a fortune to get stuff done. It's amazing.

'Any *real* printing I send out to a real printer, little bloke around the corner, called S. Wilkinson Son and Nephew. Well, it's not as snappy as Fotokwik, is it? Anyway, I keep him pretty busy round Christmas with smart invitations. Lots of people give parties, so lots of people want printed invitations with gold letters or copperplate or crinkly edges, it's quite sweet, really. And expensive. A bit for him, a lot for me.

'What did I do at Christmas? Well, work it out for yourself. I went to lots of parties. I always keep one invitation for myself out of each batch, so there I was, fixed up with about twenty parties in fifteen days. I really don't know how I stood the pace.

'Only disadvantage was, I never knew anyone at these parties, so I always had to start from scratch again. Well, that's not quite true. There was one chap I was always bumping

97

into – smart little fellow in a bow tie and velvet jacket, quite a raver. Amazing how he was at every party I went to, almost like telepathy. So I eventually went up to him and said: How come we are always at the same thrashes together?

He gave me a queer look and said, 'I thought you didn't recognise me. I'm S. Wilkinson, your printer.'

The Wrapping Paper Manufacturer

'I just make wrapping paper. Christmas wrapping paper. I make it and people buy it. That's all.

'I spent Christmas on my yacht in the West Indies. Moored off my island. I flew out there in my plane.

'Yes, wrapping paper's been good to me.'

The Christmas Sales Man

'I started queueing for the sales about three days before Christmas. Not one of your big sales; it was actually outside one of my local shops, a delicatessen where they usually have big reductions on things after Christmas, like cakes and boxes of chocolates, etc. Well, quite honestly I've got all the three-piece suites and fur coats I can handle from previous sales.

'Anyway, the shop was open right up to Christmas Day so I was getting a bit in the way and the police moved me to wait next door, which was a building society. Trouble was, they closed the delicatessen on Christmas Eve and put up a big notice saying "Closed for Annual Winter Holidays till Jan 8".

'Well, I didn't want to wait that long so I decided to queue at the building society instead, where I was still first in the queue. Trouble was, when they reopened on Dec 29, they weren't offering reductions on anything so you could say it was a bit of a wasted wait. On the other hand, people were very kind to me and made sure I was well provided for, and that's never happened before at Christmas, so you could say I didn't do badly. Might do it again next year, as a matter of fact.'

The Building Society Manager

'Christmas was absolutely ruined for me, I'm afraid. We had a report that a suspicious man had been hanging around outside my building society branch – just sitting there day after day – so I had to go round every day and keep an eye on him from a distance. I told the police, of course, but they weren't interested. It meant I just couldn't get any Christmas shopping done, except in the delicatessen next to the building society.'

The Delicatessen Owner

'Christmas was quite good, except for the odd types you get

hanging round. First, there was this man on the pavement outside in some sort of political demo, but I got the police to move him on. Then there was another bloke, pin stripe suit and bowler hat, came in every day to buy more stuff. Said it was for his Christmas presents. Likely story. All I can say is, a lot of people were surprised to be given garlic sausage and cottage cheese this Christmas. It got on my nerves eventually and I decided to close the shop for an impromptu holiday till Jan 8. I mentioned it to the police, but of course they didn't want to know.

The Policeman
'I had a good Christmas. Lots of people came to me with complaints but I didn't want to know. I was saving my strength for New Year's Eve.'

The New Year's Eve Reveller
'My New Year's Eve was pretty normal. I dressed in totally unsuitable clothes for the weather and went down Trafalgar Square about eight with some mates. First we climbed to the top of this big tree and threw ourselves off. Then we climbed to the top of a fountain and threw ourselves in the lower basin. Then we looked for BBC blokes with microphones in their hands and threw them in. Then a policeman came along and threw me in a van and I don't remember any more after that. I woke up in Charing Cross Hospital on Jan 6 with the worst of the pneumonia over, but three ribs still broken.'

The Delights Of Literature

About ten years ago *The Times* rang me up and asked me to join their distinguished crowd of end-of-the-year reviewers and name my Book of the Year. Very flattered (especially as the only thing I'd ever reviewed for them was jazz in disreputable clubs which I'm sure *Times* readers never went near) I said yes. It was only later that I realised I'd only read one new book in the entire year, Benny Green's first novel, *Blame it on My Youth*. Luckily, it was pretty good, so I nominated it. But word obviously got around literary quarters that I couldn't be relied on to nominate the latest Booker prizewinner or something by Iris Murdoch, and nobody has ever asked me a similar question since.

Till last month, when Richard Boston (editor of the handsome literary monthly *Quarto* - advt) rang me to ask what books I was reading at the moment.

'None,' I confessed. 'When you rang I was actually playing the piano.'

'At bed-time,' said Boston. 'I am asking lots of writers what books are actually on their bedside table *at this very moment*. And no cheating, lying, or moving books to your bedside while I'm talking to you.'

Luckily, the two top books were quite respectable. One was the *Selected Letters of Oscar Wilde*, out from the library, and the other was a secondhand Penguin of a *Maigret* story. *Maigret* is all right, because Simenon has a pretty high reputation at the moment, so you don't have to worry about owning up to reading him as you might worry about, say, Ian Fleming or Forsyth. It should really have been Dick Francis, as he is the most 'in' thriller writer at the moment, but Simenon was good enough.

What I didn't tell Boston was that there were twenty other books on my bedside table, all of which I have started but not finished. It's a huge, semi-occupied skyscraper of books, like a literary Centrepoint, and before the year ends I have sworn either to finish them all or blow them up like an unwanted block of flats. They actually stand higher than the lampstand. Halfway down is a huge paperback called *100 Multi-Coloured Facial Tissues*, which turns out to be a trapped box of paper hankies. I don't suppose I've blown my nose for three weeks.

And yet I started them all with high hopes and, in most cases, was enjoying them tremendously. One of them is a fascinating life of George Augustus Sala, a forgotten Victorian journalist. Fascinating, because apart from all his adventures, it shows that journalists a hundred years ago did all the things that they do today: get drunk too often, miss deadlines too often, promise to do too many articles, get involved with hopeless new magazines, go in hiding from the Inland Revenue ...

I remember now. I stopped reading that book round about the time I got a terse note from the tax people. Well, here's another: *The Dippers* by Ben Travers. I picked this up because it was the only novel, I think, written by playwright Ben Travers. Very funny stuff, too. At least to the end of Chapter 3, which is as far as I got. Perhaps it was because I then went on to *Sip, Swallow* by A. P. Herbert. I've started a modest collection of humour books of the past, and this is a collection of pieces from the 1930s by A.P.H. They're good, and nice and short, short enough to read one at a time while you're shaving, which probably explains not only the blobs of shaving cream on the book but the faint scars on my chin.

This big hardback is *Gorki Park*, which presumably I bought with my own money. It's the sensational thriller which is actually set in Moscow and features a real Russian policeman. I would have finished it by now except that just after I bought it I met the famous thriller expert H. R. F. Keating at a party and mentioned it to him. Yes, it's quite good, he said, but there's another Moscow police novel coming out next week which is even better – you should read that. Well, I've forgotten the name of the one he recommended and I really feel I ought to read *Gorki Park* first. But the thought of that other one keeps hanging over me. I haven't actually started *Gorki Park* yet.

I almost finished *A Good Man in Africa*. I passed it by to begin with, in the shop, because I thought it was *A. Goodman in Africa* – something to do with Lord Arnold Goodman and the Zimbabwe settlement. But no, it's a new first novel by William Boyd which all the reviewers said was wonderfully hilarious. It's certainly well written, but I found it intensely depressing. There's a school of comic writing starting with *Lucky Jim* and coming down through Tom Sharpe, which assumes that the more disasters happen, the funnier it is. I disagree heartily. *Lucky Jim* is funny because the disasters are all small-scale, but once they start piling up like car crashes in an American comedy film, they become as boring as – well, as car crashes in American comedies. The only thing that made me laugh in Boyd's book was the moment when the hero, reacting to the one generous impulse he has in the entire book, gives a pound note or the African equivalent to a mad looking beggar in the street. The beggar looks at it with lunatic eyes, then puts it in his mouth and eats it.

The Best of Jazz 2 by Humphrey Lyttelton is very good, but it's the sort of book you read tomorrow night when you will be able to concentrate more. *A High Wind in Jamaica* – ah, one of the great books there. So I'm told. I haven't started it yet. I don't even remember getting it. Hold on – it's one of my daughter's books. She left it there because her pile was getting too big. *The Sea The Sea* by Iris Murdoch. I discovered at about page 20 that I don't actually, really, honestly, sorry about this, enjoy Iris Murdoch terribly. So I could get rid of it, couldn't I? Yes, but I ought to try once more, shouldn't I?

Fat Man on a Bicycle by Tom Vernon. Now, this really is a good book, a leisurely progress across France on a bike, with the author thinking all the random thoughts that you and I wish we'd thought, and seeing all the secret corners of France that drive you wild with jealousy. It's such a good book, in fact, that I don't want to finish it at all, and I'm taking slower and slower doses as the end draws nigh.

And good God, what is this? *The Stage Favourites Cook Book*. Oh yes, I remember. I've had a bit of a crush on cookery this year, and bought one or two odd volumes. This one was printed in 1923 and contains favourite recipes from all the famous actresses of the time. Sold like hot cakes, I expect (see Mary Pickford's recipe for hot cakes). The awful and sad thing about the book is that while most of the recipes are still pretty well-known, the actresses have all been forgotten. Sic transit Gloria Swanson. Be honest, have you ever heard of Nellie Wigley, Doris Eaton, Gertrude Kingston, Jessie Winter, Ivy Shilling, Michellette Burani, Oleander Bisque? Oh no, sorry, Oleander Bisque is a recipe.

Well, there you are, that's my list of books I've half-read this year. Unfortunately things have got worse recently. It's all because of the Simenon. The first chunk I read was the first half of the novel. But when I next picked it up I couldn't quite remember everything that had happened, so I went back ten pages to refresh my memory. And read only three pages. The next time I went back another ten pages and read three more pages. I am now actually going *backwards* through a book, and characters who were safely murdered two weeks ago are now alive and well again. It's all very confusing.

What I think I'll do is go to my shelves and desperately try to make space for these books, by throwing out books I don't need. While thus browsing I will come across *Blame it on My Youth*, by Benny Green. I will get it down to see if it really was as good as I thought it was all those years. I will start reading it and find that it was. I will then place it on my bedside table for further reading, thus making the problem even worse.

Would anyone like to come round and read my books for me?

TV Superstars And Ordinary Mortals

Just before Christmas I got a phone call from a man at the BBC telling me that Barry Norman had decided to make *Film '81* his last in the series and go on to do *Omnibus* instead.

Fine, I said. Good idea. I didn't know Barry Norman was interested in politics. *Omnibus* isn't politics, he said. It's the arts. Fine, I said. I think you need a good arts programme. Though you've got the *South Bank Show* already. *The South Bank Show* is ITV, he said. Great, I said. I think ITV needs a good arts show. Why don't you do all the talking, then I'll stop making an ass of myself?

Well, he said, we haven't fixed on any one person to replace Barry Norman for *Film '82*. We thought we'd ask several people to do a small batch each, and would you like to do three programmes in March?

A few thoughts chased through my mind. Would I like to see a few films in March, free? Was I free, in March? Wasn't TV Centre just down the road? Wouldn't it be crazy to turn down work? The answer to all four seemed to be Yes.

Yes, I said.

Having said which, I forgot all about it in the way that one does forget a distant event like next Christmas or the dentist. So I was a bit nonplussed when people started coming up to me and saying: Oh ho, so you're going to be a TV personality, are you?

A *what*? I'm doing three jobs for the BBC in March and that makes me a television personality? Look, I've been doing odd jobs for the BBC three times a year for a long time, and nobody unknown ever came up to me in the street and started talking to me. Biggest programme I ever did was the Peruvian trip in the *Great Railway Journeys* series, a whole sixty minutes. Next morning I was in the Tube and I thought, if anyone ever recognises me, today's the day. Nobody even stared at me, trying to place me. After a while I was staring at people, seeing if they'd place me. By the end of the journey I was smiling and winking at them, making chuff-chuff noises. Not a sausage.

Correction: sometimes people I don't know do come up to me in the street and say Hi. They always turn out to be old friends with new haircuts or beards. Once I was approached by a very bearded man, about whom all I could remember was that he played tenor saxophone. The next day it clicked. He wasn't a jazz musician at all – he was the manager of the Woolwich who had given me my mortgage. But I can't remember who the sax player is I'm mixing him up with. (I've just remembered. He's the milkman. He doesn't play tenor saxophone either.)

I suppose what people really mean is that Barry Norman is a TV personality. Therefore anyone who replaces him, even temporarily, is bound to be a TV personality. I don't buy this one for a moment. It took Barry years and years plugging away at the same spot to become a household face, until now he *is* the bloke who does films on BBC. And for the next five or ten years he will be the BBC film bloke, even though he never does another film programme. So anyone who replaces him won't be the new guy who's doing films on BBC; he'll be the bloke who's doing Barry Norman's programme, just like Arthur Marshall is the bloke who took over from Patrick Campbell on *Call My Bluff*, and will be for a long time.

Not that I think of Barry as a TV personality. I first met him when I was on the staff of *Punch* years ago and he had just been fired from the *Daily Mail*, as I remember, so he was looking for work. He was, bluntly, unemployed. Later he always said that being fired was the best thing that ever happened to him, as it got him moving, working for *Punch*, working for the *Guardian* and eventually working for TV. I don't think he really thinks of himself as a journalist any more but I do; mention his name to me, and it isn't his telly face that occurs to me, it's the lean, brown, slightly wrinkled face strolling into *Punch* and depositing an article.

I guess if I seriously wanted to be a TV personality, I'd need a lot more than three weeks odd-jobbing next March. I'd need some brown wrinkles for a start. I'd need five years hard exposure on the same slot. And I'd need to know just how Barry Norman did the job.

Unfortunately, it's too late now. Barry Norman has finished doing *Film*, and I never once in all those years watched the programme, so I have no idea what made him such a great presenter, apart from the sparkling brown wrinkles. The only vision I have of him is as I remember him from the corridors of *Punch* ...

CREDITS ROLL UP. 'FILM '82. WITH BARRY NORMAN.'

Barry Norman enters by the door, with a mac over his arm.

Barry: Hi. I've got the article. I'll just leave it, shall I?

Voice: Yes, that's fine, Barry.

Barry leaves the room.

'THAT WAS FILM '82 WITH BARRY NORMAN.'

I guess the only chance I have of becoming another Barry Norman, really, is getting fired from somewhere, which doesn't seem too likely in my freelance life.

Confiding A Little Problem ...

Dear readers,
I wonder if you can help me with a very embarrassing problem.

You see, I am living with this fifteen-year-old girl, whom I am very fond of, but I have this unsightly brown growth and ...

I thought that might grab your attention. It's not often you find a columnist asking the readers for advice, and I do need advice, believe me. Let me explain. The fifteen-year-old is real enough, but she is my daughter and I just put her in to ginger things up, and she won't be appearing again in this piece. No, it's the unsightly brown growth I'm worried about. I keep it in the store room generally. In a large jar. It's made of peanut butter. I think I'd better start at the beginning.

As you know, it's been drummed into us over the years that it makes sense to buy in bulk. For instance, it's very expensive to buy a small packet of muesli; cheaper to get a large eco-bag. It's even more sensible to team together with ten other parents and buy sacks of the stuff at a discount cash 'n' carry, or cash 'n' pull-a-muscle, store.

Of course, most sensible of all is to go into business as a bulk muesli merchant, and take the stuff home free. (Even if by that time you'll probably be agreeing with Frank Muir. Frank Muir says that, though his children always called horse radish 'horse rubbish', the name would be better applied to muesli, as it always looks like the sweepings from a better-class stable.)

I have occasionally fallen for this line of argument. In Smithfield once, in a fit of enthusiasm, I bought a ten-pound bag of bacon, very cheap. With a few pounds still to go, the family had become as anti-bacon as the prophet Mohammed.

I once picked all the fruit off the crab-apple tree in our local square (*Farming in W11: A Handbook*) and turned it into excellent jelly. Three years later, I still have a dozen jars of the stuff and have become ashamed of giving it away at Christmas, though I have developed some really quite unusual recipes involving bacon and crab apple jelly, if anyone's interested.

Anyway, peanut butter: The children love peanut butter. I like peanut butter. Let's be honest, everyone likes peanut butter. But those little jars of Sun-Pat (smooth or crunchy? that is the question) disappear at an alarming rate. So one day in the folksy surroundings of Neal's Yard, the farmhouse set in the middle of Covent Garden, I bought this huge jar of peanut butter. Ten kilos or four gallons or twenty bushels, I can't remember now, but it was big all right, big enough to solve all my peanut butter problems till retirement age. I wouldn't actually bring the jar to table, of course – for one thing, it would go right through the table – but every time we ran out of pnb, we'd just decant a little more. Like having your own barrel of wine, you know, or a cow.

There was one problem I hadn't reckoned on. Bulk, economic pnb doesn't taste the same as good old Sun-Pat. No worse, no better, just different. Bulk pnb is sort of, well a bit oily and a bit dry, though it's absolutely crammed full of goodness and is very peanutty, I give you that, no question. It's just a matter of getting used to a new taste. I had just about got used to the new taste when a deputation arrived to see me, headed by the fifteen-year-old girl with whom I was then living and who has somehow got back into this piece again. 'We, the undersigned,' was the gist of their petition, 'appreciate your efforts to cut down on household expenses by buying in bulk, but we would like to point out that this peanut butter is really gross compared to Sun-Pat, which is ace, and we are definitely not going to eat your yucky big jar any more, no way, guy.'

I was in a quandary here. On the one hand, their attitude was all wrong and needed a quick crackdown for the sake of discipline. On the other hand, I completely agreed with them. So we compromised. They went back to Sun-Pat while I struggled on with the healthy, natural bulk pnb, which is so good for you, also heavy, hard to handle, greasy, disgusting and depressing, so we reached a further compromise i.e. we all ate Sun-Pat.

And that is why I have this huge jar of peanut butter in the store room and why, dear readers, I am asking you if anyone out there has any good ideas for using up the stuff. Preferably in large helpings. Or for crab apple jelly, come to that. Or indeed for muesli, of which I seem to have more than I realised ever since the younger generation discovered that it was more fun and cheaper to mix your own nuts and raisins and bits of apple.

'Morning, children. Anyone like some peanut butter on their nuts and raisins?'

'Get lost, dad.'

I once acquired a recipe for peanut cookies, which involved using pnb. Very good they are, too. Full of peanut taste.

Unfortunately, the peanut taste comes mostly from the peanuts you have to chop and shovel into the cookie mixture; you're only allowed to use 1oz of pnb, and it's going to take me another seventy cooking sessions to get through that lot, and anyway the children have gone off peanut cookies now, especially when spread with crab apple jelly, so that's no use.

Once, and once only, I have been taken to an Indonesian restaurant, and I seem to remember that Indonesian cooking involves a lot of pnb. Could any Indonesian readers help me on this one? Any recipes using more than 1 lb at a time is what I'm after. Preferably leaving no left-overs.

Failing which I'll settle, if I have to, for advice on how to deal with fifteen-year-old daughters, though if you ask me that's not half so difficult as getting rid of peanut butter.

STOP PRESS I've just been giving the pnb its annual stir. The bottom half has solidified, as well it might after two years. Anyone got any ideas for using peanut bricks?

The Dense Undergrowth Of
The English Language

Q. Why would a person read a book with a dictionary lying ready beside him?
A. Either because he was reading a book in a foreign language or because he had just started an Anthony Burgess novel.

I have just started an Anthony Burgess novel. Actually, I've read 150 pages already which would bring you to the end of some novels, but this is *Earthly Powers*, his big, sprawling, exciting etc masterpiece etc, and we haven't really started sprawling, properly yet. Already, though, I have realised that Anthony Burgess would be great on *Call My Bluff*. He knows words that the rest of us thought Patrick Campbell had taken to the grave with him, and sprinkles them through the novel as if we knew them as well – words like supinate, brewis and omnifutuant.

I think he throws them in for fun, as a composer might write in a few bars for baritone saxophone or Hawaiian triangle; for a bit of flavour which is quite unnecessary. Brewis, for instance. What do you think that means? Well, I'll give you three meanings and if you can spot the right one, you're allowed to continue the article.

1) Bread soaked in gravy, soup, etc.
2) Hebridean word for primitive kind of sheep.
3) Boy assistant to a Catholic priest.

Got it? Of course. Bread soaked in gravy, or so I learn from the excellent new Collins English Dictionary, which is so voluminous that it is even bigger than Anthony Burgess's new novel, *Earthly Powers*. The thing is, Anthony Burgess uses the word 'brewis' at a meal set in Rome eaten by a priest and a Londoner, and brewis is apparently a North Country word, so what on earth is it doing here? It's as if the priest suddenly turned to the Londoner and told him he was gormless or doolally.

110

Supinate, by the way, means 'to turn the hand till it is facing upwards' and omnifutuant is a very rude word, meaning with sexual appetites that stop at nothing. They're nice words and I am glad I came across them, but I do not imagine for a moment that I shall ever use them in everyday conversation, for the simple reason that nobody would have the faintest idea what I was talking about. 'You naughty boy! Supinate so that I can smack you!' …'What this soup needs is a bit of brewis' … 'The next door dog is omnifutuant – he's fallen in love with my trouser leg'. Hopeless. The whole point of having words is to communicate, and if we don't use words that communicate, then they're no good.

The *Reader's Digest*, for instance, says that it pays to increase your word power. Well, it certainly pays to learn what normal words really mean. When I hear a politician or trade unionist say: 'I totally refute that accusation,' when what he means is 'I totally reject that accusation' (because refute means to disprove, and how often do they disprove any accusation?), then I feel aggrieved, cross, irascible, choleric, etc. But it only pays to increase your word power to a certain extent, just as you wouldn't want to build your muscles beyond a certain limit for fear of looking like Arnold Schwarzenegger. I met a feature in the Scottish *Sunday Standard* last year which tried to expand my word power with ten new words. I'd only met two of them before. I tried to learn the other eight, but they were so obscure and specialised that I have never met them again since, have never dared to use any of them and now can only remember two.

One is 'disembogue', which means what a river does when it comes to the sea, and the other is, 'euphuistic' (not euphemistic), meaning very flowery and ornate, of a prose style. I had to look that up just now, because I can only remember the word, not the meaning. Next door to it I found 'euplastic', which is another new one on me – means, apparently, 'healing quickly and well' of a wound. Nice, eh? Totally useless, too. Using words like that is like asking for things which aren't on the menu or dialling numbers which don't exist.

And yet, and yet, using words like that does bring colour to a jargon-ridden society. When we talk about jargon, we usually mean broken-down scientific words like parameter or interface or ongoing or viable, but fashionable trendy talk is just as

111

much jargon: no-way, hype, getting things together, really into, a downer, funk, boogie ... (A lot of pop talk, interestingly, is old jazz talk recycled. Boogie has been around since the 1920s, bop since the 40s and funk since the 50s – even hype is about thirty years old. Just thought I'd show off a bit.)

What I find specially interesting is when phrases or words survive long after their origin has disappeared. You sometimes hear people confessing to being stymied, which is the golf equivalent of being snookered, though the stymie disappeared from golf decades ago. We talk about hanging up on someone, though nobody has hung up a phone on the wall for donkey's years. Flushing a lavatory is always described as pulling the chain, though I dare say nine times out of ten we push a knob or depress a handle. And the expression doolally, which I slipped in earlier on, meaning mad, is one you still hear around, although the British Army mental hospital in India from which it comes is not one that most of us know about, and I for one can't spell it properly because it isn't in my otherwise excellent Collins Dictionary.

You often find that writers have their own favourite obscure words. Alan Coren's is 'Norfolk Howard', which means a bug. There was a Victorian gentleman named Bug who decided, reasonably, to change his name and adopted the new one, unreasonably, of Norfolk Howard. This misfired completely, because a scornful public took revenge by using Norfolk Howard to mean a bug. Peter Dickinson's favourite obscure word was 'exopthalmic', which means 'with the eyeballs visible from above', and you don't get more specialised than that. Mine, more modestly, is 'pinguid', which is another nice word for oily, greasy or fatty. And there was a character in an Aldous Huxley novel whose favourite word was 'carminative'. He didn't know what it meant, he just liked the sound of it. Ruby-red, he thought it might mean. One day he made the mistake of looking it up. It meant 'laxative'.

So where does this leave us? I'll tell you where it leaves us. It gives me a once-in-a-lifetime opportunity to write a piece of obscure prose, which I know all my readers will understand and to get a few words out of my system.

'Where the River Mbobo disembogues its pinguid waters into the sea, and the omnifutuant lobsters gambol among the floating brewis, I took a paddle. Not for long, though, as contact

112

with the waters made my hand smart. I supinated, and saw a euplastic wound on the palm of my hand. "You're doolally to go in those waters," said a friendly if exopthalmic passer-by. "They're riddled by disease. Spread by Norfolk-Howards," he added helpfully. Stymied, I retreated on to dry land, but the effect of the water must have been carminative, for I found myself asking the way to the nearest lavatory. "You can use mine," said the friendly stranger, "as long as you promise to pull the, I mean, press the, that is, activate the flushing mechanism."'

Not a great bit of prose, but you've got to admit it's euphuistic.

"She Hated His Guts":
A Complete Romantic Novel

Esther suddenly realised she had no idea how old Mr Grant was.

Up to that moment he had simply been the man who gave her letters to type out, people to invite to lunch, phone calls to make, letters to type out again. But one day she found herself noticing the silver hairs behind his ears. Attractive, in a sort of way. There were silver hairs inside his ears as well. Men were going grey much earlier these days. She also began to notice the way his mouth crinkled when he smiled, which he did whenever he gave her letters to type again.

'Only two f's in effervescence,' he would say, and was that the ghost of a wink?

Yes, for over a year she had taken him for granted. Now that she began to study his little ways, and the easy masculine style with which he approached her, her attitude changed. She started to loathe him.

God, how she hated him. She hated the way his perfectly cut clothes fell over his perfectly cut figure. She hated the attractive suggestion of lemon sorbet given off by his after-shave. She hated

113

the way one untidy lock of hair fell over his forehead, making him look so uncommonly boyish yet grown-up. Above all, she hated the way he did not even seem to notice her.

And still she had no idea how old he was. Twenty-seven? Thirty-seven? Forty-nine and three-quarters?

What's more she didn't care.

'The way you go on about how much you hate Mr Grant,' said her flat-mate, Stella, 'worries me, you know.'

'Why?' said Esther, ironing a blouse.

'It suggests to me that you really quite fancy him.'

'What nonsense,' said Esther. 'If I hated him, I wouldn't go on about how much I fancied him, would I?'

'No, so what?'

'Well, that proves I do hate him.'

'That may be so,' said Stella, feeling she'd missed a link in the argument somewhere. 'When are you going to wear that blouse?'

'To the office tomorrow,' said Esther, blushing unaccountably.

'That's a nice blouse,' said Mr Grant. He had never commented on her clothes before. But Esther wasn't taken in – she knew it was just part of his general charm-school approach to life. Still, she felt she ought to make an answer of some kind.

'How old are you?' she asked, before she realised just what she had said.

Mr Grant wasn't fazed at all by the question. A man who is in deep trouble with the Inland Revenue has faced far worse questions than that.

'Old enough to remember dancing with your arm round your partner and young enough to prefer the other sort,' he said. One side of his face smiled while the other stayed still. He did it better than Robert Redford. God, she loathed him.

'Esther,' he said unexpectedly.' I should have taken you out to lunch years ago. I'm really meant to be eating with old Robinson, the chairman. But today I want to have lunch with you.'

If she said yes, much against her will, it was only so she could spurn his advances. And, of course, put him in bad odour with Mr Robinson, who was not in her eyes old at all but really rather nice.

It was while the main course was being cleared away that he suddenly made his pitch.

114

'You know, Esther, you and I have a lot in common.'

'Oh, yes,' she mocked, despite herself. 'We are both very attractive people and have no ties and could have a nice time together and be damned to what the office says.'

Mr Grant looked genuinely surprised.

'Heavens, no. I don't consider myself particularly attractive and you're certainly not. No, I meant that you and I are the only two who know all the details of our Swiss banking operation.'

Startled, Esther found herself listening to a plan for defrauding the company out of about £200,000 which would need the combined ingenuity of both of them, plus a trip to Zurich under assumed names. About to reject the whole idea out of hand, she suddenly realised that Mr Grant was treating her, not as a woman, but as a person. A colleague. A partner, even if in crime. *As an individual.* He needed her, yes, but for her knowledge and expertise, not for her blouse.

'All right,' she said. 'I'll do it. But what do we tell the bankers in Zurich when they ask for customs guarantees ...?'

It worked even better than she could have expected. The flight to Zurich was pleasant (she had never seen the Alps before and thought they looked every bit as good as in the colour magazines), the hotel was the best she had ever stayed in and the bankers fell for it, hook, line and sinker. She had thought the Swiss hotel people might have thought it suspicious when they booked in as Mr and Mrs Trotter, and then asked for separate rooms, but they were apparently used to English couples. Now she sat on her bed, counting out £100,000 and mentally saying good-bye to her cold flat life in Shepherds Bush for ever.

'Well?' said Mr Grant from the doorway.

'You were very good,' she said. 'The way you convinced Herr Zügler in the bank that the firm needed the cash for immediate government bribes – well, you did it superbly.'

Then he did a shocking thing. He crossed to her bed and threw her money on the floor.

'I don't care about the money. That's only incidental. It's you I want.'

'I don't understand, Mr Grant.'

'*Please* stop calling me that. I am Chris. And I want to stay

115

here, in this room with you. May I, Esther?'

Suddenly she saw everything.

'The ... the job was just a blind, wasn't it? You fooled me all along. You made me think I was important to you as an economic colleague, as a partner. But all the time you were just giving me financial sweet talk – oh God, you were treating me as a woman!'

'Esther, *please!*'

'Stop!'

The voice came from the doorway. They both whirled round. There stood Mr Robinson, the chairman.

'I am surprised,' said Mr Robinson. 'I am even shocked. That you could have trapped this innocent into your cunning scheme. Luckily, I found out in time, but I shall never quite understand the kind of power that a woman has over a man to drag him down like this. Are you all right, Chris?'

With a kind of rising panic, Esther realised that the chairman was blaming *her* for everything and that he was gazing softly at Mr Grant. But, before anyone could reply, a new arrival erupted into the room.

'Chris, Chris, I came as soon as I could! Oh my darling, am I too late?'

It was Stella. Stella, her flat-mate. Stella, rushing across the room and throwing herself into Mr Grant's willing arms. This was terrible. Everyone was against her. And everyone seemed to be in love. They were all gazing at each other with a nauseating, mushy, vegetable adoration. Only she was sane. She was caught in some kind of monstrous nightmare. Oh God. Oh Mills, Oh Boon.

'This is madness!' she shouted. 'Look, let's go right back to the beginning and start all over again, and let's get it right this time!'

Esther suddenly realised she had no idea how old Mr Grant was.

Up to that moment he had simply been the man who gave her letters to type, or to type again. But now she found herself noticing the silver hairs behind his ears. She recognised the danger signs and, to comfort herself, patted her handbag to make sure that the small silver-handled pistol was in there. This time she would be ready, no matter what happened.

116

The World's Grosser National Products

I earn a somewhat precarious living writing a daily piece for *The Times*. You know, big serious newspaper. When you pick it up, supplements on Bahrain fall out. All the best bits – letters, personal ads, etc – are written by readers. That's the one. Rupert Murdoch has been threatening to close it down recently. You've got it. I shouldn't really be telling you this, but it was actually a gimmick to put on circulation. People who normally wouldn't touch it bought *The Times* every day, thinking that each issue was going to be the last and therefore a collector's item. It put millions on the circulation. Clever, when you think about it.

Anyway, the other day I wrote a piece to celebrate A. A. Milne's centenary, which gave some of the more unusual names Winnie the Pooh is given in foreign translations. Ole Brumm in Norway, Micimacko in Hungary, that sort of thing. One was the Swedish title which I copied down from the publisher's list – Winnie Nalle Puh.

Well, this morning I got a letter from a Swedish reader living in Tunbridge Wells, pointing out that in Sweden he was known simply as Nalle Puh, because Nalle meant teddy bear already and they didn't need the Winnie bit – something like that – the point was, as she said, that the Swedes were very thorough so she felt she *had* to make the point. 'Yours pedantically', she signed herself. I got the point all right when the next letter I opened was from a Swedish man (living in Weybridge) saying that in fact in Sweden they didn't use the Winnie bit and that Nalle already meant little bear …

I really don't want to force this Winnie the Pooh bit down your throats – the point is that quite by accident I have received good documentary evidence about the Swedes which I shall be able to use some time in the future. When you get *two* letters in one breakfast about the Swedish word for bear, then you certainly are dealing with a pedantic nation. I'm glad I got two letters because now I can send them each other's letters and they can start a pen pal thing between Weybridge and Tunbridge, or even meet each other and hate each other at first sight. But it started me thinking about this national character thing.

Last year, for instance, I noticed that the Gate Cinema in Notting Hill was showing *Death in Venice* as a late-night film, but that through some misunderstanding they had advertised it as 'Deaf in Venice'. So I wrote a short screenplay for this unknown film about a deaf composer in Venice, in sort of sub-Woody Allen vein, and thought no more about it till last week when I got a letter from an English teacher living in Germany. He, apparently, had given my piece to his class as an example of English humour (God bless you, sir) and at the end of term had asked them all to write something about a piece that appealed to them. One girl promptly turned in a 1,500 word essay on my 600 word piece, analysing what I was doing and telling me things I didn't even know about myself ('Kington here is operating on two levels of reality simultaneously ... ' Oh yeah? I thought it was just cod Woody Allen.)

The point being that only the Germans could take humour so seriously, or bother to analyse it. Peter Ustinov once imitated a German joke-telling: 'First I will tell you about the joke I am about to tell. Then I will tell the joke, after which I will explain it, and then you may laugh.' There are, I am proud to say, no famous books written by Englishmen explaining humour, only by Continentals.

Just to complete the picture, I got a furious letter the other day from a Scotsman complaining about a piece I'd written, which took the mickey out of some aspects of Scots culture such as getting drunk, selling tatty tourist tartan rubbish, sending armies of football supporters abroad and thinking that Andy Stewart is the greatest thing on two legs. My piece had been reprinted in the *Scots Independent*, the organ of the Scot Nats, and they had added the comment: 'Substitute the word Paki or Jew for Scot, and you could send this to the Race Relations Board.' My anonymous correspondent had further compared me to Julius Streicher, the Nazi Jew-baiter of the 1930s. Well, quite apart from the fact that the Pakistanis don't send tartan-clad football yobboes abroad and that Jews don't think a great deal of Andy Stewart, I felt that this reaction was a little strong so I comforted myself with the thought that the Scots *hate* being criticised by the English. The only people who are allowed to tear the Scots to bits are the Scots themselves.

What I'm getting round to is that, racialism or no racialism, national characteristics do exist, and to deny them is crazy. You can't begin to understand the Afghanistan situation till you realise that the Afghans have nothing special against the Russians – they've gone around shooting *anyone* from outside for centuries, including the British, and killing their neighbours when there's no one better on offer. You don't begin to understand Soviet Russia itself until you realise the strength of passion which ties Russians to their motherland, Communist or not. You can't understand the French mind till you realise that they believe in principles whereas we believe in practice. That's why they are so keen on writing new constitutions and why we don't even have one.

That's also why the rest of the world persists in believing that the English are hypocrites. As circumstances change, we change our reactions, but the rest of the world only sees us being shifty and untrustworthy. That's also why we find Mrs Thatcher so unnerving – she has actually announced a principle and stuck to it at the cost of being hated, and we really don't know how to react to it, apart from hating her for it.

Of course, there is another reason for the English being thought hypocrites, and that is that *we are* hypocrites. I'm sorry, but we are. One of the great problems about the ASLEF dispute is that everyone *knew* that train drivers sometimes skived off, sometimes moonlighted, had to have other jobs, weren't always there when they were meant to be there. The workers knew, the management knew – but they had to pretend they didn't know. Everyone knows that management skives too. The odd thing about British hypocrisy is that it cuts both ways; sometimes we pretend we are working full-time at a job whereas we are really skiving off, sometimes we pretend we are working full-time at a job whereas we are really working full-time at two or three jobs. The black economy, the cash-only-squire world, the doctor who treats a farmer free in return for a side of beef, is all part of the same thing.

What I've always wanted to do is write a book which got

119

down on paper all these national characters the world round, if possible through the kind of stories that people tell about each other – the French about the English, the Turks about the Greeks, and so on.

In fact, to be quite honest, I have actually got round to agreeing to write such a book.

In fact, to drop all my natural English hypocrisy, that's why I wrote this piece. To ask you readers – Swedes, Scots, Germans, just plain English – to send me any enlightening experiences you may have about national characteristics. I'd be grateful to hear from anyone. Cash only, of course. Used 10p coins probably. No need to tell the tax people about it. Wink, wink.

Agony in the Upper Circle: A New Hercule Ustinov Thriller

'*Evil under the Sun* may be the last Agatha Christie film we make' – film company statement.

'Come in, mesdames and messieurs. Please seat yourselves so that we can get on with this regrettable business. Lady Darcy, you will be comfortable here.' Hercule Ustinov, the most famous film detective in the world, ushered the aged film critic to a chair. Lady Darcy could hardly see or hear now, but her ability to sum up a film from the press hand-out was as legendary as ever.

'Sir Leslie, perhaps you would sit over here?' Sir Leslie Judd, the distinguished film director, raised his eyebrows briefly and walked to the chair designated, where he sat with a slightly flouncy gesture that one associates with gays of the old school. In fact, he was as normal as an old tea cloth, but he had been around actors so long that some of it had rubbed off. Sir Leslie had won many awards, especially in the last year or so. Most of them were honorary ones to make up for the fact that in previous years he hadn't won many, but he enjoyed receiving them, and selling them off a week later. Things were not too good with the Judd finances.

Next to him sat the young actor, Charles Landor. Landor was very handsome indeed and people were waiting to see if he had any brains to go with it. There was no sign either way so far. Next to him sat the young starlet, Diana Perkins. According to rumour, she and Charles were having a passionate affair. Charles was quite happy with the rumour. In fact, he had started it himself. As to whether there was also an affair, nobody was saying. After all, they were both happily married to other people.

There were seven other people in the room, but we shall not describe them one by one otherwise we shall be here all day. Also, research shows that the average reader cannot remember more than about four characters at a time. Rest assured we shall introduce them as and when it becomes necessary, in a most painless fashion.

'I think we all know why we are here,' said Hercule Ustinov, when everyone had seated themselves. All eyes were fixed on his face, and so was a large moustache. It had started to peel at one corner. Ustinov replaced it with a twirl.

'Last night we were all present at a film preview. To be precise, of my new film, *Execution in Paradise*. We were there for two hours. We were all there at the start and all there at the finish. But during those two hours *one of you sneaked out, travelled a mile through the London traffic to commit a crime and came back again.* Yes, one of you here. The question is, which?' Ustinov looked out under his heavily made-up eyes at all present.

'That's ridiculous, Ustinov,' said Lady Darcy sharply. 'We were all here. No one could have gone out unnoticed.'

'Allow me to correct you, madame. Anyone could have gone out. During the film, all is rapt. There is great attentiveness. We glue our eyes to the screen. It is very easy to sneak out and back. And you would not have noticed, my lady, because you were asleep throughout.' Lady Darcy snorted.

'It is true. People do not snore when they are awake. Do you remember me going out?'

'No.'

'And yet I did. I visited the gentlemen's toilet. Alas my bladder is not what it was.'

'You Frenchmen all drink too much,' said Charles Landor.

'Belgian, monsieur. I am a Belgian, and I do not drink. But when I was in the, what does one say now, loo, I noticed Sir Leslie's jacket hanging up there. And not just his jacket, but also his coat and trousers. Now why, I ask myself, would Sir Leslie Judd wish to change during a film?'

'Absolute rubbish,' said Judd hotly. 'It was very warm in the preview cinema. Just thought I'd take a few clothes off. Nothing odd about that.'

'And you, Charles Landor,' said Hercule Ustinov, ignoring this. 'I happened to notice that you were wearing a hat, and dark glasses, and scarf.'

'Yes,' said Charles. 'Bit of a chill. Had to wrap up. Doctor's orders.'

'I suppose you remember the moment when the film broke down and the lights went on?'

'Er, yes – yes, I do. Damned nuisance.'

'Not to you, Mr Landor. I happened to notice, during the sudden light, that although your hat and scarf and dark glasses were there, *you were not in them*. It was a dummy, Mr Landor.'

'Oh, but that's absolutely ridiculous ...' Hercule Ustinov proceeded to prove with unnerving logic that everyone had left the cinema at one point or another, often for long periods, and that any one of them could be the culprit. When he had finished, there was a long silence.

'And so you see,' said Hercule, 'that ...' He was never to finish the sentence.

'Just a moment, Ustinov,' said Charles Landor. 'We have something to say to *you*. Isn't that right, everyone?' They all nodded, except Lady Darcy, who was fast asleep.

'It is true that we all left the cinema. But you have not mentioned the reason why. *We* have not mentioned the reason why, because we are too polite. But now that you have insisted on talking about it, I have to tell you that none of us could bear to watch another Hercule Ustinov film right through.'

Hercule's mouth fell open, and his moustache wobbled.

'Yes, monsieur, the *real* crime took place up there on the screen. Another two hours of torture – of motive-building, of alibi-constructing, of interrogation. No wonder we all had to go out and do *anything*. We just could not face another Agatha Christie all-star vehicle. My God, we are all artists! To have to

face *that* ...' His voice broke with emotion. About time too – he was already twenty-four.

'And now, to have to sit here this evening and go through it all again. It is more than flesh and blood can bear.'

Hercule Ustinov's mouth opened and closed, saying nothing.

'If you really want a *proper* crime,' said Sir Leslie.

'If you really want a murder,' said Lady Darcy, waking up unexpectedly.

'Then we can provide it,' said Landor.

Hercule Ustinov suddenly realised that they had all got to their feet and were coming towards him.

'No!' he cried. 'Non, non, messieurs ...'

Two minutes later it was all over.

The great Belgian film detective had appeared in his last feature.

(This article is shortly to be made into a major movie.)

The Greasy Spoon Awards

(Strange, isn't it, how the *Good Food Guide*, *Michelin* and all those restaurant critics never go to the places *we* go to at lunchtime? Here at last is an authoritative gourmet guide to London lunch places which fills a long-felt gap, and that's more than can be said for most London lunches.)

Our inspectors visited four unidentified establishments which between them cover the lunches taken by 99% of the population. The result would have been exactly the same if the visits had taken place in the City, Oxford Street or Knightsbridge, as these establishments seem to be part of nationwide chains.

The Sandwich Bar is probably the most popular of all four, as a large queue forms outside its doors at 12.45 and does not disperse till 1.25. The ambiance is friendly; a large family of Italian origin stands behind a wide glass case and discusses personally with each customer what he would like in his sandwich and what colour bread he would like it on. Advice is certainly needed, as the bill of fare promises a dizzying selection of combinations, from beetroot, Stilton and peanut butter to liver sausage, gherkin and anchovy. Perhaps this is why most customers seem to play safe with ham or cheese.

The decor is based largely on posters for Heinz tinned soups, though these are not, as first thought, Andy Warhol reproductions, but personal gifts from the Heinz company. 'They very good to us like that,' explained Luigi, the head sandwich maker, who has recently moved here from the Bromley Sandwich Mart. 'Also the Pepsi people very nice. They give us our outside name.'

I chose egg and anchovy on white with mayonnaise (48p) while my companion opted for the prawns in coleslaw on a white bap (70p). The ingredients were taken from small white trays by the head maker's very own fingers and thumbs, which were slightly scented with salami. My sandwich, which came with a free napkin, piece of greaseproof paper and a white paper bag, was delicious, but my companion pronounced the prawns a bit tasteless. Luigi admitted that they were in fact not fresh from the market that morning, though recently thawed, but said that the English on the whole did not like their prawns to be strongly flavoured. 'They come back and say, what this fishy taste? It must be off.'

There is a short but worthy beverage list ranging from Pepsi (25p) to tea (17p), and a wide selection of crisps. You can phone in advance and then queue to collect your order. Lunch for two came to £2.16.

Still very hungry, we went next to *The Café*, a small steamy establishment run by a small steamy Italian family. Chef Alfredo, who has recently been tempted there from the minicab firm he was running which went bust, told us that he had at first tried to feature Italian dishes from his native Manchester, but had encountered consumer resistance, and now had settled down to a popular repertoire of English dishes. 'We serve breakfast at breakfast time,' he explained. 'You know – egg, bacon, sausage, beans, chips – all that thing. These are lightly fried in our own frying pans, using our own fat. Then at lunchtime we served breakfast all over again. This we also do once more at teatime. This the English like.'

My companion chose tonna e fagioli, while I plumped for fresh noodles in sour cream and mushroom sauce. We both got egg, bacon, sausage, chips and beans. It was excellent, though the sausage tasted somewhat of bread. Alfredo said that this was because the English do not like their sausages to taste of meat. For dessert we asked for spotted dick and steamed pudding, but both got bowls of lumpy custard. It was excellent.

The ambiance is intimate, to the point where it is hard to tell which table you are sitting at, though there is no question of overhearing the next person's conversation as nobody speaks, except the staff who maintain an unbroken argument in Italian about the foolish engagement entered into by an unidentified niece. Those who object to canned music may dislike the constant Radio 1; when we asked for it to be turned down, we were told that it had been on so long nobody knew where the switch was. Lunch for two came to £3 plus tip, say £3.10.

Having left most of our lunch on the plate we were still

hungry and so adjourned to the *Kebab, Pizza and Burger Place*, a very popular establishment featuring international cuisine. The chief feature of the place is a huge lump of minced meat on a spit circulating in front of a gas fire, which has the effect of drying the meat on the outside and leaving it pink inside. When it is too dry, slices are carved off and left in a small metal warmer. They are then placed inside a flat piece of bread together with a slice of tomato, some unwanted lettuce and a squirt of red sauce. This is called a donner. Or a burger. Or a pizza, if the ingredients are placed on top of the bread. It is a traditional dish from Italy, Turkey and New York City. We asked the chef for his recipe for the red sauce, but he did not speak English.

To assuage our hunger we finally visited the *Crossed Keys*, part of a vast chain also known as the Red Lion, Marquis of Granby, Green Man, etc. Most of the premises are devoted to the sale of drink (they have an extremely good if expensive beer list) and food is only sold from a glass counter behind a pillar next to the Gents. Two kinds of food are on offer; dishes cooked inside a cellophane bag and food not cooked inside a cellophane bag. The chef, who is also married to the man who sells the beer, was honest enough not to recommend the cottage pie, which she said had gone a bit dry, but after all it was after two o'clock. The goulash and rice was excellent, she said, but all gone, similarly the macaroni cheese. She said why not give the steak and kidney pie a whirl? Or the Cornish pasty? Or even the pork pie if we were feeling strong. My companion opted for the pasty and I for the steak pie, which are distinguishable by their shapes. Both dishes had an extremely generous helping of pastry, which unfortunately left little room for the insertion of the filling, which unfortunately was gravy. Yes, said the chef, they weren't the greatest were they but what could you expect these days and anyway don't forget we were getting as much free salt, pepper, mustard, ketchup, brown sauce, and relish as we liked, not to mention some bits of cellophane which had become dry and attached to the pastry, she was sorry about that. Lunch for two was £1.75 not including beer.

We ate standing up from a shelf which was not quite wide enough to take our plates, as all seats and tables were occupied by people who had lunch breaks from 12 to 3. The chef

126

explained that this was now quite normal on a Friday. They would all go home straight after lunch to avoid the weekend rush hour. Decor was homely and provided by a bewildering array of postcards sent from customers on holiday, small bull-fight posters, bills of foreign currency, pennants of visiting darts teams and small cards which claimed that one should not ask for credit as a refusal frequently offends, and also that one did not have to be mad to work there but it helped. We asked the chef how long it took to collect this treasury of popular British culture and she said, about half an hour, the brewery had put it all in to make the place seem authentic.

We then ended our afternoon at my companion's flat where, among other things, we cooked a delicious omelette which we ate with a large glass of red wine. Cost for two, she said, was nothing.

Great Jeans of History

Sir James Jeans. The English scientist after whom jeans are named. To clear up any doubt on this matter, turn to the Encyclopaedia Britannica where it is stated that James Jeans was born in 1877 and at Cambridge, in 1898, became the second *wrangler.*

He is famous for the discovery of all sorts of scientific processes, but above all for the discovery that a hard-woven mixture of cotton dyed blue made an excellent pair of trousers capable of standing up to the most abrasive laboratory bench in Cambridge. For his work in the field of denimwear he was awarded in 1924 the Nobel Best Dressed Scientist of the Year Prize.

Jean Gabin. Something like the gabardine, the jean gabin was a waterproof denim cloak invented in France and often used in films of the time where the hero was featured in canal barges, by the River Seine, sailing to America on the Titanic or in other situations likely to involve drenching.

Denim Elliot. A later English version of the jean gabin. Denim elliot was a good, workmanlike, dependable cloth featured in many British films of the1950s and 1960s, many of which are now shown on television long after we have all gone to bed. There was even at one time a denim film studio on the A40 out of London.

Jean Plaidy. A curious Scottish attempt to cash in on the denimwear market, jean plaidy was a tartan denim cloth based on historical models, a strange cross between jeans and the kilt. The wearer tended to resemble a Scottish football supporter in drag and never really caught on. There was a fashion for a while for a model for Scottish teachers, called the *jean brodie.*

Jeannette Macdonald. An even odder version of the above, a Scottish version of the Bermuda shorts. Jeannette Macdonald can most politely be described as an aberration of the 1930s which did not deserve to survive – and didn't.

Jean Arthur. There were many attempts to popularise different kinds of jeans in the early days of films, of which jean arthur was the best known. The last one of any note was *jean simmonds,* a demure version of jean arthur, but female jeans for some strange reason died out in the film world; *norma jean* was so unsuccessful under that name that it was immediately redubbed *marilyn monroe* twill, and did rather better.

Jean Borotra. Wimbledon tennis was dominated between the wars by a quartet of dashing Frenchmen known as the Four Deuces. One of them, Borotra, was highly suspicious of the English weather and devised his own all-denim tennis suit for use at Wimbledon, known as the jean Borotra. The Wimbledon rules committee were deeply suspicious of this garb, which they considered ungentlemanly, but after a three year search could find nothing in the laws of tennis against it. They did however gain a compromise insofar as they persuaded him to go without his denim beret during the second week. None of the foregoing is to be confused with that cut-price retailer *billie jeans king.*

Jean Renoir. Renoir probably used the most extravagent colours of all the Impressionist painters and gave his name to the line of French jeans which came in six different glowing huges: purple, crimson, lemon, charcoal, puce and montélimar. (There was no choice; they *all* came in six colours.) At the first jean Renoir fashion show the critics jeered at these daring creations, but Renoir had the last laugh – an authentic jean Renoir is now worth anything up to £500,000. (For those Frenchmen who could not stand the brightness of hue, a dull sandy-coloured jean was developed later, the *jean sablon*.)

Jean-Paul Sartre. The only truly philosophical jean ever invented. It was a French concoction, though based heavily on the works of Marx and other heavy thinkers. The idea was to develop something so thick, so impenetratable, so incomprehensibly durable that it would stand up to almost any treatment. The French are very fond of revolutions, being invaded by the Germans and other national catastrophes, and jean-paul sartre has come successfully through many of them; it showed great resistance during World War II and proved just as popular in the May 1968 uprising. It was going strong until very recently.

Jean-Claude, etc. The French have experimented heavily in recent years with the artificial mixing of jean with other synthetic materials and have produced such fabrics as the *jean-claude brialy* (a tweedy mixture), *jean-belmondo* (elegant cocktail outfit) and *jean-louis trintignant.* Although popular at the time and much featured in films, none of them has quite retained a grasp on the public imagination.

Jeanson. A curious postscript to the French scene. Jeanson was for many years an obscure French thinker (all French thinkers are obscure, but he really was), and remained in obscurity until the late 1970s when some bright spark divided his name in two and made a smash hit record out of it. Subsequent efforts to do this with names like Bergson, Jackson and Timpson have all failed abysmally, which seems to show there is something special about jeans.

Jean Rhys. An even more obscure attempt by the Welsh to cash in on the denim boom, jean rhys was a sombre, closely-knit, almost unobtainable, semi-waterproof garment. It has now been replaced by the *angharad rees*, a welsh anorak.

The Maturest Student Of Them All

This year the Open University celebrates its tenth anniversary, and so do I. Of course, the celebrations are for the granting of the Charter in 1969; it's stated in the books that 1971 was the first year in which students were taught. This is not quite true. I started in 1969. I simply wrote a letter of inquiry to the University and was deluged in return with the material for four different courses, weighing a total of 17 kilos.

I had not really thought about becoming a student (my letter was actually written to complain about the invasion of Radio 3) but it seemed too good a chance to miss. I chose a Technology course on *Mass Production*, as at the time I had invented a self-righting egg cup for use at sea, and was tired of making them by hand.

I had completed the course by 1971. I made the mistake to begin with of writing far too long essays. Not only did this bore my tutor rigid, it also cost a great deal to post and I ran up huge bills with the Post Office. My final essay, though, was a masterpiece of clarity, being only one sentence long. Here it is. 'Making procedures more sensitive to individual needs usually involves making them more complicated and hence more expensive and thus prone to error.' This gained me a ninth-credit. I was a little taken aback later to find my sentence reprinted without credit in *How to Study*.

By 1972 I had made 40,000 egg cups and sold 300.

My next course was in *Medical Technology*, as I had devised a plan for converting egg cups into eye baths and was interested in getting a fat contract with the NHS. This I had achieved by 1974. Unfortunately, in 1975 I was failed the course. I appealed against the decision, stating that anyone who gets a fat contract with the NHS cannot be totally a failure. The appeal was upheld and I was given a credit. Also, the

130

resident medical staff at the OU ordered three eye baths, for which I gave 10% discount.

After ten years as an OU student I am often asked how I fit in study with my family. My answer is that I do it the other way round – I fit in my family with my studying. Many students make the mistake of getting involved in family life before enrolling – I enrolled first, then married and had a family whom I trained to revolve round my hours of study. They actually think that that is how I earn my living. It was for a while, in fact, as I set up a profitable wastepaper firm selling all the literature I received from the University.

In 1976 I received a polite reply to my 1969 letter about Radio 3. I also started a course in the *History of Logic*. I was somewhat surprised to get as my first essay subject this topic: '"Making procedures more sensitive to individual needs usually involves making them more complicated and hence more expensive and thus prone to error." Discuss the logical fallacies contained in this statement.' This I took to be an attack on the TMA system. I wrote a long and thoughtful essay agreeing completely with the statement. I then wrote another tearing it to shreds. I had 1,000 copies of each privately printed and sent them all to my tutor with a note: 'Enclosed please find 2,000 essays mass-produced to make them less complicated, less expensive, hence less prone to error.' After a long gap I received them back. His note said: 'I have marked the top copy of each. The other 999 are marked by resolution. Congratulations.'

By 1977 I had acquired three credits, one ninth-credit and a half-credit which had been lost in the computer. Owing perhaps to the same computer error, I had also become the member of 17 book clubs, which gave my wastepaper firm a much needed boost.

The disadvantage of being a long-term student is that you change mentally and physically. I now disagree totally with most of what I thought, wrote and said ten years ago, and have sometimes toyed with the idea of returning my early credits, like the Beatles sending back their MBEs. If I had my time over again I would do things very differently. I would, for instance, have converted my egg cups into ball-and-cup toys for children.

One year I was at summer school in Oxford, and I asked one

131

of the old college porters about the difference that age made to students. What about the undergraduates who had done National Service first, for instance, and came to Oxford older and wiser? 'Oh, they were very different,' he said. 'They had a much higher standard of practical joke. I remember two of my lads in 1949 who'd been in the commandos. They blocked the dean's staircase with a barbed wire entanglement. He was up in his room all day. They were the only two who knew how to remove it, you see.'

You don't get that sort of thing at the OU.

I am no longer a wastepaper merchant in my spare time. I am a TV producer. This came about recently when I was looking for new courses to study. I rejected things like *Man's Religious Quest, Science from Religious Quest, Science from Copernicus to Darwin* and *History of Mathematics* because Bamber Gascoigne, James Burke and others were doing perfectly respectable TV programmes from which I could learn as much as I needed. Or had they – I suddenly thought – been students of these courses themselves and then turned them into TV? *And why didn't I?*

One day a BBC producer came to our regional centre doing one of those dreary items on the kind of people who study with the OU. The taxi driver, the policeman – you know the sort of thing.

'And what do you do?' he asked me.

'I'm a TV producer,' I said.

'Really?' he said, somewhat startled. 'Who for?'

'Well, I haven't started yet,' I admitted. 'But I'm doing a course on *The Revolutions of 1848* to turn into a 13-part TV series called *The Year Europe Nearly Died*. I think I'll get Frank Muir to front it.'

'A super idea,' he said. 'Come and see me when you've got a script.'

I've been to see him and the series has now almost been finished. The beauty of it, of course, was that the research was all done for me by my tutor.

So the first ten years have been quite a success for me at the Open University, and I look forward to another happy ten years. Trouble is, I now have almost enough credits for a degree, which is the last thing I want, as I might be required to move on.

Still, if I do get another credit, there is still the appeal system to fall back on. It shouldn't be too hard to lodge an appeal against my credit and get the result overturned and changed into a failure.

In Praise Of Useless Information

Trying to explain the peculiarly British nature of Monty Python, an American writer once told his American audience that it was partly due to the habit of British universities stuffing their pupils with useless information. It wasn't strictly necessary, for instance, to know about Marcel Proust or Jean-Paul Sartre, but these six English lads did know about them; hence the appearance in Monty Python's Flying Circus of the 'Summarise Proust in Fifteen Seconds!' contest or the shouting matches between Parisian housewives labelled Mrs Sartre, Mrs Camus, etc. This sort of thing just wouldn't happen in America.

He was right. The only American comedian I can think of who uses useless information is Woody Allen, who sometimes drags in scraps of Freud or existentialism. The English love useless information, far more than any other nation. That's why we love quizzes, whether on TV, in the Christmas newspapers, or in the pub. That's why our crosswords are the hardest in the world, depending on a severe knowledge of geography, literature and science, not to mention a twisted mind. That's why it was us, not anyone else, who came up with the Guinness Book of Records.

Where I disagree with the American is in classifying all this as useless knowledge. Using it in crosswords, Monty Python, even daily conversation, makes it immediately worthwhile. I am all for useless information; it's colourful, irrelevant, interesting and appealing. You can't have enough of it. What you can have too much of - and we have *far* too much of it - is useful information.

133

Useful information is all the statistical analysis on the side of cereal packets. (1.4 mg of Riboflavin per 100 grammes, etc). It's the credits at the end of films or TV programmes. ('Assistant to the Wardrobe Mistress: Cindy Birdbottom'.) It's the biographies of the actors in a West End theatre programme. It's the result of the 1981 Census. It's the *Sunday Times* telling us that at 9.05 am on Thursday April 30 President Reagan got into his size 10 shoes, took his two daily boiled eggs and turned to the sports pages, as he always did. It's statistics, measurements, back-up data, in-depth breakdowns, more statistics. It's any briefing that isn't brief.

Useful information on the back of a long vehicle, for example, would be a sign telling us that the vehicle is 17.6 metres long, 3.4 metres wide and 5.6 metres high. Some genius, thank God, has ditched all that useful information and put a sign on saying LONG VEHICLE. That is all we need to know.

Useful information is telling us the likely temperature in the next 24 hours in both Centigrade and Fahrenheit, and getting it wrong in both.

What we should be told is: 'The temperature will be average for the time of year, but will feel colder because of the north-east wind.' That's what we *really* want to know.

Useful information, except in very small quantities, is useless. It gets in the way. Who was it said 'I want to sweep aside the facts and get at the truth'? I don't know (it's useless to know, really) but he was right. All through my adult life I have read, at five-year intervals, that a new set of bones has been discovered in Africa, older than anything known before and upsetting all our previous ideas on the origins of man. I have not taken in the new theories attached to these bones, partly because it makes little difference to me whether our ancestors walked or used tools first, partly because it never settles anything. The important and only really useful fact, which no one ever mentions, is this: 'Every five years someone discovers a new set of bones which upsets all known theories.' Even more briefly: 'There will be another skeleton along in a moment' - just as we know that sooner or later the Treasury will confess to an error that invalidates all previous calculations, or the estimates for the new motorway or space satellite have to be doubled owing to the discovery of a new skeleton in someone's financial cupboard.

What makes it all worse is that the saturation of our lives with useful information gives us a false feeling of confidence that someone somewhere has got all the answers. Therefore we, personally, do not need to know. Therefore, as information increases, we ourselves know less and less. I used to love those stories I read as a boy of some modern character being transported back to the Middle Ages and showing the amazed medievals how to build a wireless, make a car or organise a unit trust. I now realise that fewer and fewer of us actually know enough, in our own brains, to do these things. We would have to have our data retrieval systems transported back with us.

The chief symptom of our almost religious belief in useful information is our urge, every time something goes drastically wrong, to set up a commission to look into it. A commission, in other words, to collect so much useful information that nobody has the slightest idea, or much less idea than before, what to do about the problem, the only hope being that in the years it takes the commission to collect all available useful information, the problem may have either gone away or been labelled as insoluble.

So bully for useless information, I say. I don't mean statements like 'All the inhabitants of the world could stand side by side on the Isle of Wight' or 'Every day a forest the size of Rutland is chopped down'. That's merely useful information boiled down to the consistency of a government health warning or scare headline. I mean *really* useless information. Like that the country in the EEC with the highest proportion of teetotallers is (guess? go on!) Ireland. Like that the only Hollywood star who had previously been awarded the Iron Cross for fighting on the German side in the Great War was (any idea? you'll never guess) Rin Tin Tin. Like that if you leave bits of raw white fish in lemon juice, it cooks it. (Old Peruvian recipe, since you ask. Fascinating, eh?)

I prefer useless information because you can be sure of it. Useful information, beyond the bare minimum, is so unreliable. I have almost given up reading financial columns now, because I know that after the opening blast of useful information about the many kinds of insurance policies, or mortgages, or pension schemes, there will come a point when the writer says: 'However, the kind that is most useful for you depends on

135

your personal circumstances and it is best to consult an expert.' In other words, he abdicates just when he has got through the useful stage to the really useful stage.

The late great Groucho Marx had the right attitude to useful information. He once was taken to a spiritualist seance at which the medium finally got through to the other side. Had anyone got any questions? What a chance! To find out if there really is an after-life, and if so whether to dress casually for it or not. To ask who is going to win the 3.15. To find out how Dickens wanted to end Edwin Drood.

'Yeah,' said Groucho. 'What is the capital of South Dakota?'

Or, as Fats Waller said when asked what rhythm was: 'Lady, if you got to ask, you'll never know.'

What I think I'm trying to say is that if it's in a statistical table, it's probably not worth knowing. The only really useful information we ever pick up is what we learn *despite what we are told*.

A Beginner's Guide to Peru

(Important note. This is not a guide for beginners to Peru. It is a guide written by a beginner to Peru. It is believed to be the first of its kind.)

Geography
Peru is a large country on the west side of South America which contains all of Peru as well as parts of Chile, Bolivia and Colombia, though the maps do not show this. It is divided into three parts; the coastal strip, which is so dry that nothing grows there, the sierra, which is so high and cold that agriculture is impossible there, and the selva, which is so fertile that it is not yet under cultivation.

The population is about 17 million, of whom about 16.9 million live in the capital, Lima, where they are employed selling each other things in the street. The main products of Peru are blank cassettes, ear-rings and snacks (see Food). Lima must once have been a very fine town – indeed, every traveller who has visited Lima in the last four hundred years has commented on this fact. Research is under way to find a traveller so early that he comments on how fine a city Lima is, but so far he has not been found.

The capital of Lima is Miraflores.

Climate

There is no climate in Lima, only a sort of light drizzle. This lifts from January to May to reveal that Lima must once have been a very fine city. At the end of April summer is officially declared closed and nobody ever goes to the beach thereafter, except a few foreigners who can't believe their luck in finding such warm water and sunny beaches.

In the mountains it is hot by day and cold by night. Whereas Europeans protect themselves against the cold by closing

137

windows, doors, etc., the inhabitants scorn such soft habits and merely put on more clothes. Any highland restaurant at about 10 p.m. is filled with citizens eating dinner in overcoats, gloves, scarves and woolly hats, with the wind roaring through the room. This is known as machismo; there is no cure.

During the winter it rains all the time, though this season has been renamed summer to attract more tourists.

History

Peruvian history is divided into three main sections: the Inca Empire, Spanish domination and the War of the Pacific (1880-1980).

The Incas were a fierce but well organised people who forced their subject tribes to build some of the most impressive ruins known to mankind. The Inca masons had to build their stonework entirely without cement or mortar, and even today supplies are still pretty bad, but thousands of tourists flock annually to Macchu Picchu to see the Inca remains; many of them, it must be admitted, tour the unfinished Macchu Picchu Hotel and leave under the impression that they have seen the real thing.

The Spaniards were a fierce but well organised people who tricked the Incas into believing that they had come as tourists. While the Incas were still filling out the immigration forms (see Bureaucracy), the Spaniards massacred them and proclaimed, in the most high name of the Spanish king, the setting up of the Peruvian Gold, Silver and Nitrate Corporation. This was finally overthrown in 1824 by a series of liberators called Plaza San Martin, Hotel Bolivar and Saint Bernard O'Higgins, all of whom retired disillusioned unable to master the paperwork entailed by independence.

Peru grew briefly rich in the nineteenth century after the discovery of remains left by the Guano tribe and thus attracted the attention of their neighbours, the Chileans, a fierce but well-organised people. The Chileans invaded Peru and, after a fiercely contested war lasting several years and millions of paperbacks, were declared the winners on points; in the ensuing peace treaty, they won the right to export apples to Peru in perpetuity. The Peruvians have always claimed that the result was a fix and demanded a replay, but their messages to the Chileans have so far remained unanswered. (See Communications, Difficulty of, in South America).

Today Peru has settled into a peaceful cycle of democracy followed by unrest followed by military takeover followed by unrest followed by democracy. It is best to check with your hotel clerk before you go out which state has been reached at the moment. NB: in Bolivia, next door, this whole process takes place within twenty-four hours.

Communications, Difficulty of, in South America
Owing to the altitude, climate, distances, etc, letters always experience great difficulty in getting through and often expire before arrival. If visiting Peru, you would be well advised to write and send postcards before you leave home. If doing business within Peru, the normal practice is to pop round to your correspondent and read the letter to him. Do not forget to make three copies (see Bureaucracy).

Time Difference
Peru is six hours behind Britain, thus giving rise to the common fallacy that Peruvians always arrive six hours late for appointments.

Politics
There are three ranks in the Peruvian Army: Private, General and President. Most soldiers rise quickly to the rank of General, but it is comparatively rare to become President, unlike in Bolivia where all generals become president. The head of the Peruvian Army lives in the Government Palace in Lima, guarded by soldiers who goose-step up and down at approximately 0.3 kilometres per hour. Some historians consider that this may explain Peru's coming second in the War of the Pacific.

Currency
The Peruvian currency is based on the 'libra', though all coins and banknotes are marked in 'soles'. This is part of the national sport of Fooling the Gringo. (See Sport). Similarly, all coins are virtually identical but with different markings. Banknotes are divided into two sections, but may easily be joined again - it is said that Peru is the only country in the world

where sticky tape is legal tender. First-time visitors to Peru may be surprised that banknotes are so faded. This is because they are washed so often. The banknotes are made of 80% rayon, 20% cotton and should be handwashed every three or four days at a temperature not exceeding 60°C.

All transactions should be conducted in the exact amount, as Peruvian traders never seem to have change; they do in fact have change, but it is hanging out to dry.

Roads

Peru has the most modern roads in South America; this is because they are washed away each winter by the rains and replaced by new ones.

The majority of motorists in Peru drive on the right. It is permissible to drive on the left if:

1. There are more of you going your way than coming the other way.
2. There is a pot-hole, pile of sand or flock of llamas on the right.
3. You are overtaking a car driving at the same speed as you.
4. You feel like it.

When traffic lights turn red in Peru, it is considered courteous to slow down.

At an intersection, right of way goes to the larger vehicle; at a level crossing, right of way goes to the train.

If you intend to have an accident during your journey, it is necessary to fill out a form beforehand. (See Bureaucracy).

Although not legally obligatory it is thought polite to hoot continuously if you see another car.

Main Towns

The main town of Peru, as distinct from the capital, is the town you happen to be in at the time. It is a matter of proven historical fact, for instance, that Arequipa is the finest, most important and most influential town in Peru. The same goes for Cuzco, Huancayo, Trujillo, Piura etc, which are all still very fine cities as opposed to Lima.

Altitude

Many first-time visitors to Peru may experience difficulty at altitude in converting metres to feet, as the exchange rate varies constantly; this leads to headaches, dizzy spells and over-charging by the natives.

Other effects of altitude include:
- Boiling an egg for eight minutes
- Watching your bottle of beer froth all over your trousers.
- The train leaving late.
- Letters not getting through.
- Bureaucracy (see Bureaucracy)

Food and Drink
Visitors to Peru are often advised that, to avoid illness, they should avoid taking any food or drink in the country. Although this does wonders for the figure, it often leads to faintness, malnutrition and death. In fact, Peruvian cuisine is very fine indeed and can be safely indulged in as long as the following basic rules are kept in mind:

1.   Anything with the letters -ch in it is almost certainly an exotic native dish, from choro to cebiche to salchipapa. Really exotic dishes have two -ch's in them, such as chicharrones, chicha and chancho. Anything on a menu that does not have -ch in it is almost certainly beef; puddings all begin with -p (pie, panqueque, postre).*

2.   Do not ask for gateau. You will be served with cat.

3.   Chicha is a native drink made out of maize, potatoes, rice, cotton, straw, mud, adobe, egg and monosodium gluta-mate. It tastes not unlike cold Ovaltine. People who like cold Ovaltine will go for it in a big way.

4.   Peru is a snack-oriented country. At every street corner there is a small kerosene burner on wheels surrounded by three chairs, at which you are welcome to sit and partake of the speciality. Do not ask what the speciality is. It might spoil the experience. Peruvians eat snacks all day long, breaking off only to drink fruit juice, wipe their lips with napkins and look for another snack stall. The great attraction of snack stalls to Peruvians, of course, is that it is the one place where they don't have to fill in forms or get permits (do not see Bureaucracy).

Bureaucracy
See Sport.

*So, to make things more confusing, does poultry; pavo, pollo, pato …

The Indians

There are two schools of thought about the Indians. One is that these small dark hill-dwellers are lazy and unreliable and speak in a barbaric language out of sheer perversity. (Exactly what the English say about the Welsh.) The other is that the Indians, on the contrary, have a fierce independence, a wonderful gift for music and a unique culture. (Which is just what the Welsh say about themselves.) The only tentative conclusion one can draw is that the Indians would probably be fantastic rugby players.

Sport

The main national sports of Peru are Fooling the Gringo, Bureaucracy, and wondering what the hell the Bolivians are up to now. The most popular undoubtedly is Bureaucracy, a game for about 5,000,000 players in which the object is not to win, not even to take part, but above all never to finish. It is an entirely professional game: amateurs never even get to the starting-line.

Vin Extraordinaire

Just over a hundred years ago, the wine-growing world was swept by a terrible disease called *phylloxera superintellectualis*, which means wine snobbery. It has never really gone away again. You may easily find yourself sitting at table next to someone with this awful ailment and have to deal with it. You may even have it yourself. In either case, it is best to know enough about wine to display the correct symptoms. These following notes, based on a lifelong interest in studying the effects of alcohol, usually in experiments on myself, should get you through the darkest hour.

The year: It is often said that the year is very important for drinking wine. This is absolute nonsense. You can drink wine

any year you like. If I thought I had to wait until the end of
1982 before I could open a bottle of wine, I would seriously
think of transfering to beer.

The sommelier: French word meaning a wine waiter; from
the word '*sommeil*' meaning 'sleep', as he is usually dozing
when you need him.

The bottle: Very important. Wine that does not come in a
bottle, but in a large brown plastic barrel marked BRITISH
WINE – GREAT NEW CONTEST! – LOTS OF PRIZES is
not a serious wine. Recently, plastic bottles have started
coming on the market. Most wine-lovers sneer at them. If,
however, you feel you are liable to drop bottles on the way
home from the off-licence, they are a remarkably good
investment.

The label: Very important. A bottle that does not have a label
is not a wine to be trusted. It may not even be wine. It could be
that old wine bottle you kept olive oil in, or some of that

home-brewed detergent you thought had been finished off at the last washing-up party you threw.

The cork: Most important of all, as it is the last area not invaded by wine snobbery. If in doubt what to say about wine, especially when asked to comment on a freshly opened bottle, tap the cork, sniff it and take a bit off with a fingernail. Then say, 'It's rather a young cork, isn't it?' Or 'This cork hasn't been treated terribly well,' or even, 'I rather fear this is cheap Algerian cork.' One mustn't always be condemnatory, of course. From time to time exclaim: 'This is truly one of the great corks of the world!'

The label again: The label should give you all the information you need – who printed it, what ink, the typeface and so on. Generally speaking, the more words and initials there are, the better the wine. '*Vin de pays*' is not as good as '*Vin délimité de qualité supérieure*'. Worst of all is '*Vin.*' The best wines are called 'AOC'. A wine marked 'A-OK' is boastful American growth.

Sparkling wine: There are basically three kinds of fizzy wine. There is 'sparkling', which makes a slight fizzing noise in the bottle. There is '*pétillant*', which after about three hours makes a fizzing noise in your ears. And there is '*mousseux*', which leaps out of the bottle on to your trousers.

Scientific background: According to a recent book on wine, 'the wine will have retained some oxidation from the air which it absorbed while it was stored in cask. This oxygen together with that in the small pocket of air underneath the cork takes hydrogen from the very small quantities of the ethyl alcohol to produce acetaldehyde. From this, small traces of acetic acid are formed, and the interaction of the acids and alcohols produces the esters which impart to the matured wine its aroma and bouquet as well as its flavour and smoothness.'

Now, there are two things you can do about this. One is to memorise the whole passage and frighten your fellow diners within an inch of their lives. More usefully, you can use bits and pieces from it almost indefinitely. 'Not enough esters, I reckon.' 'Do you think the acids and alcohols have sufficiently interacted?' 'Jolly little acetaldehyde, isn't it?' Don't forget: if in doubt, or in panic, demand to see the cork again.

Another diversion can be created by murmuring, 'Poly ester? That's Miss Rantzen's liittle girl, isn't it?'

144

Binning: After it is all over, don't forget to put the bottles in the bin.

Wine talk: Wine people talk about wine as if it were a middle-aged woman. It can be dull, full-bodied, coarse, hard, silky, soft, tough or unctuous. Don't bother to learn all these terms. Nobody knows quite what they mean, only what they feel as if they might mean. Invent some of your own. Try and think of wine, for example, as a young man.

'Bit gruff, isn't it?'

'I find this wine a little argumentative.'

'It's quite a handsome young wine, but it doesn't have a single idea in its head.'

'What this wine needs is a damn good spanking.'

'I'm going to take this wine outside and throttle the living daylights out of it.'

Or as your granny.

'Not bad for its age?'

'Still gets around quite well, considering.'

'I think this wine should have stayed at home on a night like this.'

'I don't think we ought to alarm the others, but I think this wine is dead.'

Emergency Action: If all else fails, and there is even someone at the table who knows more about cork than you do, try rising to your feet and proclaiming: 'Of course, where this wine is made, they think that drinking it from glasses ruins it.' Then grab the bottle and drink the whole lot down. I always find this creates an immensely strong impression.

Coronation Mall S.W.1.

The scene is a large palace in London, at the bottom of Constitution Hill. Well, it's not that large. I mean, it's not as large as nearby Westminster Abbey or even Stag Place, the office tower block, and nobody even lives there, only comes in during the day. So when people criticise Buckingham Palace as being too large for just a few people to live in, they should remember the even larger places where nobody lives at all. Is that understood? Right.

In this palace live a middle-aged couple. They are our monarch and her husband. They are sitting together in the drawing room after supper. Or drawing together in the sitting room. Either will do.

Queen: I think it's too big.

Duke: What?

Queen: The palace. It's enormous, and hardly anyone lives here.

Duke: It's not that huge.

Queen: Even the forecourt is huge. By the time you've gone to pick up the milk from the gate in the morning and walked back again, it's usually gone sour.

Duke: Well, it's not as big as Westminster Abbey or Stag Place, and nobody even lives there. (*Author's note: I know we've had this argument already in the introduction, but the people watching this on TV won't know that. Or that the Queen has different ideas about it from me.*)

Queen: I still think we ought to move somewhere smaller.

Duke: That would be impossible.

Queen: Do you think we couldn't get a mortgage?

Duke: No. I think we couldn't get an Act of Parliament. And you've got to admit it's very convenient for opening Parliament, trooping colours, beating retreats and all that.

Queen: (*sighs*). Yes, I suppose so. (*She starts humming.*)

Duke: (*leaps out of his chair and stands up*). I wish you wouldn't do that!

Queen: Do what?

Duke: Hum the National Anthem.

Queen: Sorry dear. (*He resumes his seat and goes back to 'The Daily Telegraph'.*) What gets me down is that it's so very quiet now. Since the children left, I mean.

Duke: It wasn't that noisy when they were here. They always made their noise in another wing. Anne could have ridden horses down her corridor and we wouldn't have known.

Queen: Gosh! That might explain the marks in the carpet and the funny smell.

146

Duke: Still, you're right. It *is* quiet without them. Anne in the depths of Mudshire. Charles choosing curtains for his new house or going to Welsh evening classes again. Andrew bombing around in helicopters. And then there's Edward ... where *is* Edward? One wonders what he'll be up to soon.

Queen: Jesus.

Duke: I *beg* your pardon?

Queen: Jesus College, Oxford. That's where I hope he'll be going.

Duke: Mmmm ... It's pretty grand, isn't it, naming your college after Jesus? Can you think of anything half as grand?

Queen: I can think of something three times as grand. Trinity College.

Duke: Nice one, Queen. (*A pause.*) Shall I turn on the nine o'clock news?

Queen: What on earth for? It's always so depressing. Especially when somebody says that Her Majesty's Government is determined to do something, and I can't even understand what it is they are trying to do.

Duke: Don't worry. Nobody else does either. No, it's not the news I'm after – I just thought we might see the children on it. You know, Andrew rescuing someone in a helicopter or Charles opening something or Anne falling off ...

Queen: We agreed – no more jokes about falling off horses.

Duke: Sorry. It's just that, as they have so little time to write, it's about the only way I can keep up with what they're doing. See what Diana's new dress is like. Look for Charles' hand signals.

Queen: Hand signals?

Duke: Didn't you know? Well, you know Charles and I both stand and walk with our hands behind our backs? The thing is, you can do it in several different ways; clasp your hands together, hold your right elbow with the left hand, hold the left elbow and so on. They all mean different things.

Queen: Like what?

Duke: Can we go yet? This man is boring – please, someone, rescue me. I have forgotten this lady's name. That sort of thing.

Queen: How childish.

Duke: Not at all. It's saved my life several times. (*Long pause.*) We could get out a video.

Queen: Not the wedding again!

Duke: Not the wedding again. Sounds like one of those books.

Queen: What books?

Duke: Oh, nothing, nothing. (*Pause.*) Shall I get out the photo album?

Queen: I'd rather not. You always manage to get the private detectives in the foreground. Or get me from behind.

Duke: When I'm always walking a few paces behind you, I don't have much choice. (*Pause.*). Did I tell you that Jimmy Young has asked me to go on his prog again?

Queen: Will you go?

Duke: Mm. I think so. The money's not great, but it's fun.

Queen: *I* never get asked to go on.

Duke: Well, it's different with you, dear. Anyway, you've got your own programme, at Christmas time. On all channels, too, I may say.

Queen: Don't remind me!

Duke: And you never have guests on *your* programme. Maybe if you got Jimmy Young on, he'd ask you back to his.

Queen: I think you're being a bit flippant about a rather important subject.

Duke: I wouldn't say Jimmy Young's prog is that important.

Queen: (*glares but says nothing*).

Duke: It would be nice if one of them phoned.

Queen: One of who?

Duke: The children.

Queen: Mmmm. I've told them they can always reverse the charges from Australia or wherever. Trouble is, the operator never believes them when they say their name is Prince Charles. (*The phone rings and the Duke leaps over to it.*) Hello? Who is it? Pardon? (*He puts his hand over the receiver and turns to the Queen.*) Are we Paddington train inquiries? (*She shakes her head.*). No, I'm afraid you've got a wrong number. Is there anything I can do to ...? Oh, He's gone. Pity. Sounded quite nice.

Queen: Are we Paddington train inquiries indeed!

Duke: Well, the Palace has so many departments these days, you can never be sure. Man rang up the other day trying to sell me a horse. I sent him packing. Turned out it was one of the equerries trying to get through to the mews.

Queen: We are not a mews.

148

Duke: Nice one, Queen.

Queen: Do stop saying that!

Duke: Yes, dear. (*Pause.*) It would be nice if someone just dropped in. Wouldn't have to be one of the children. Anyone – a duke or earl or somebody, popping in to pass the time of day.

Queen: Oh, yes. Unfortunately, it's not that easy just to drop in at a palace. It's all right in an ordinary house – just ring the bell and say, we've dropped by. Here you'd have to run the gauntlet of half the army. Even then you'd probably get pinioned to the wall by some over-zealous police officer.

Duke: Police do a good job in damned difficult circumstances.

Queen: Yes. I like Sting best, personally.

Duke: Nice one, Queen – oh sorry!

Queen: Did you know there was a pop group called Queen?

Duke: Heard about it the other day. Saw a poster for a record called Queen's Greatest Hits. Got quite a shock. Didn't know you'd been cutting a few tracks. Was quite relieved when they told me it was a group.

Queen: Why don't you put a record on?

Duke: There isn't really much choice. It's either regimental marches or anthems of all nations.

Queen: What about that samba record the President of Brazil gave us? We never listened to that.

Duke: It was made of gold, unfortunately. Had to go straight in the vaults.

Queen: Oh dear. (*Pause.*) It's so quiet without the children.

Duke: Mmm.

Queen: I really think we ought to move to somewhere smaller, you know.

(*At this point the reader should go back to the beginning and start again.*)

Vin Litéraire

All wine articles are the same; only the labels are different. I first learnt this when someone unwisely asked me to be among the judges for a wine and food writing contest. I knew nothing about wine and food, so I just judged the writing. And one thing I discovered is that when wine writers go to that darling little vineyard tucked away in a place that you and I will never get to, they all write the same article. I have combined the best elements in one fruity but surprisingly light article. When you have read it, you will never have to read one again. Even better, I will never have to write one again.

The little-known wine-growing area of Vendange lies somewhat south of the main Burgundy district, near the modern town of Beaujolais Nouveau, and it was in the small village of Bouquet-les-deux-Bouchons that I was privileged to meet Maurice Mineur, whose family have produced wine in the same *vignoble* for hundreds of years. Together with his son Patrick, his daughter Isabelle and their goat Rachmaninov, they tend 14 hectares of land (about 60,000 bottles) to produce the delicate white Moncracher wine for which the area is noted – not to be confused with the famous Montrachet.

Spring is particulary beautiful in this part of France, with almond blossom everywhere, especially on the almond trees, and the delicate scent of eglantine in the hedgerows. It was with a sense of anticipation that I drove up the flinty, dusty track that leads to the Mineurs' ancient farmhouse, where I found the family already hard at work eating breakfast. This consisted of warm *brioches* straight from the oven, crusty French farm butter and a huge bottle of wine.

'This wine is my children,' said Maurice, swirling a small amount round his glass and smelling it tenderly. I noticed, fascinated, his technique of dipping his bushy moustache into

150

the wine, sniffing it appreciatively and later wringing it out into a small bucket, for nothing is ever wasted in wine-making. 'To me, each bottle is different. I can tell just from the introduction of my nose where each one is born. This one, for instance, she is from a chalky vineyard facing east. You can tell from the sniff.'

He took a large helping and drank it all down. Patrick took up the tale.

'Our approach to the wine-making is traditional. Not for us the new machinery with the press buttons and the flashing red lights. Still we use the old wine press and the operation by hand and foot. It takes longer but it is worth it. We are still working on last year's harvest, actually, but you must not hurry wine. Wine is like a woman – she is never ready when you want to go out for an evening.'

He too took a large glass of Moncracher and Isabelle continued the tale.

'My brother is a male chauvinist pig. That suits me well, though, for as his sister I shall never have to marry him. A little wine?'

She handed me the bottle. Not seeing a spare glass, I raised the bottle to my lips and took a large draught. They clapped their hands and laughed.

'I see you English know how to treat a good wine,' twinkled Maurice. 'Now it is time to show you my little estate.'

The Mineurs' farmhouse, hundreds of years old, is a large, shady building covered with tangled ivy, creeper, nasturtiums, roses and, on the south wall, a huge poster for St Raphael. Beneath the farmhouse are large cellars which have housed bottles for hundreds of years, except during the War when they housed up to five hundred fleeing RAF officers at a time.

'*Mon Dieu*, they could drink,' reminisced Maurice. 'During the day they would work for me in the fields and at night they would open the bottles and teach me their traditional drinking songs. *Gringo the Russians Oh!* is the one I liked best.'

'And in 1945 they all went home, I suppose,' I hazarded.

'Not so,' said Maurice. 'They had drunk so much that they owed me wages and many of them had to stay till 1947 or 1948 to work off the backlog. They were good days.'

The Mineurs' vines grow on chalky soil, which gives to the resulting wine what can only be described as a chalky taste, which is not unpleasant but comes as a surprise if you are used to a grapey taste.

'This is what I would call a not successful bottle,' said Maurice. 'Look at the overseas bodies.'

Looking closely, I could see that the bottle contained large quantities of chalk, a few flints and what looked like a twig. Maurice knocked it angrily against a tree and it broke.

'My wines are my children and from time to time I must spank them. Now here is a *good* bottle. A little sampling?'

I tasted it over and over again until I could begin to appreciate its truly noble, flinty, redolent character. Patrick meanwhile was explaining to me the technical nature of wine production with many figures and statistics, while I took notes as best as I could, considering I was also wrestling with a large bottle, a stick of warm French *pain* and some *paté* fresh from the pig. Referring to my notes now, I see I have written: 'It is odd to see someone like Patrick with a handlebar moustache and a neat blue blazer. I wonder if his father was a passing squadron leader?'

The French laws of inheritance demand that each plot of land is parcelled out between the children, so that vineyards tend to grow smaller and smaller. Within a mile or two, Maurice told me, there are no less than 800 different *viniculteurs*, all cousins, which means that there are considerable traffic jams on market day. On the other hand, you are never short of a fourth for bridge. When Maurice dies, the land will have to be divided between Patrick, Isabelle and a certain Wing Commander Bentley of Farnham in Surrey, about whom they never talk. But what will Isabelle do with her share of the property?

'I will continue to grow wine as we have for hundreds of years,' she confided. 'Maybe I will marry, I do not know. We are so remote here that I do not meet many men. In fact, you are the first man I have seen for a good long time. Will you write often when you go back to dear old England?'

I must confess I had not paid much attention to Isabelle hitherto, but whether it was the effect of the wine or the warm spring weather, I found myself suddenly attracted to her grave, chalky eyes and flint-brown moustache, which glowed softly in the French sunshine. Over lunch, which was an impromptu affair of beef casserole, roast pheasant, fresh salmon and

152

home-grown vegetables, with another bottle each, I could not help reflecting that the life of this simple French family was nearly ideal.

'Must you be going off so soon?' said Maurice after we had wiped the last remnants of gravy from our plates with crusty French napkins straight from the laundry.

'Alas, yes,' I said. 'I now have enough material to churn out a 1,500-word article and I must rush back to enter it for a food and wine writing contest.'

'Ah, you English,' said Patrick. 'Why is it that you are always writing about food and wine and never enjoying it?'

It was a question which burned in my mind as I got unsteadily into my little hired car, drove down the dusty farm track and steered accidentally into an unsuspected ditch which had lain covered by undergrowth for hundreds of years. The family found me there later in the day, fast asleep. They hospitably invited me to stay until I was able to move on. Now, three years later, I am still here, for Isabelle and I have developed a, how shall I say, certain understanding, as indeed the French have done for hundreds of years, and I look forward now to the day when our little son Rupert will in turn inherit his three and a half hectares, though at present he is obsessed only with the idea of joining the RAF about which his grandfather tells him so many stories.